HEAD VERSUS HEART
AND OUR GUT REACTIONS
THE 21ST CENTURY ENNEAGRAM

MAPPING THE DIFFERENT WAYS
WE ENGAGE WITH THE WORLD

MICHAEL HAMPSON

WITH A FOREWARD BY DR. ROWAN WILLIAMS
ARCHBISHOP OF CANTERBURY

KT-377-776

BOOKS

Winchester, UK
New York, USA

Copyright © 2005 O Books
Deershot Lodge, Park Lane, Ropley, Hants, SO24 0BE, U.K.
E-mail: office@johnhunt-publishing.com
www.O-books.net

USA and Canada
Books available from:
NBN
15200 NBN Way
Blue Ridge Summit, PA 17214, U.S.A.
Email: custserv@nbnbooks.com
Tel: 1 800 462 6420
Fax: 1 800 338 4550

Text: © 2005 Michael Hampson
Illustrations: © 2005 Michael Hampson

Cover design: Krave Ltd, London

ISBN 1 903816 92 0

A CIP catalogue record for this book is available from the
British Library.

Printed by in the USA by Maple-Vail.

HEAD VERSUS HEART
AND OUR GUT REACTIONS

Contents

Foreword

Written by a highly experienced, wise, and practical parish priest, this book guides the reader gently and firmly through a whole program of discovery and – in the proper sense – conversion.

This particular reader was forced again and again to recognize the challenging sense of the analysis offered, and hopes that many more will find the same excitement and prompting to growth in these pages.

Dr. Rowan Williams
Archbishop of Canterbury

Preface

Michael Hampson trained as a priest after studying cognitive, behavioral, and neurological psychology – the psychology of the mainstream scientific community.

To *Head versus Heart* he brings the insights of this psychology – along with a practical, pastoral spirituality.

The result is a powerful system for understanding ourselves and the people around us that is logical and rational throughout – and where the assumptions are the assumptions of faith: that when we speak of the experience of humankind we must speak of a spiritual journey, of gifts and temptations, and of participation in the wider community of faith.

The emphasis throughout is on the practical and the positive: the gift and the potential that each person brings, and the path from where we are now to the very best of what we are called to be.

Head versus Heart rebuilds the enneagram on a single new foundation: the fundamental question of how we engage with the world.

To this task we each bring three basic resources – "head" and "heart" and our "gut reactions". *Head versus Heart* is a study of the interaction of these three.

The concept of the "strategy" becomes central early on, so the enneagram is recast as "the strategy board," with nine "sectors" and nine strategies for the nine classic "points" of the diagram.

From the top of the first page, *Head versus Heart* explains as it describes – something that has never been done for the enneagram before – making *Head versus Heart* the most important new work on the enneagram in thirty years, and the definitive enneagram text for the twenty-first century.

Reading *Head versus Heart* is a spiritual journey in itself. Page by page it gives new insights into our own struggles and dreams, and the gifts we take too much for granted, and the things that hold us back. It helps reveal our natural spiritual gifts and our individual calling – then plots the route toward the practical fulfillment of that calling. Along the way it also makes sense of the diverse people all around us – their weaknesses, their gifts, and the struggles and spiritual journeys in which they are engaged – making it so much easier to respect them, work alongside them, engage with them, and value their gifts.

While the language here is that of mainstream Christian spirituality – temptation and redemption, "the seven deadly sins," biblical heroes, different patterns of prayer, "participation in the body of Christ" – there is plenty here for people of any faith or none. *Head versus Heart* is a personal journey of discovery – built on the common experience of what it is to be human in the world.

Introduction

"The strategy board" provides a map of the whole of humankind, and a map of the spiritual journeys we make. It can show us where we are, and where we have been, and where we might go. It can help us to understand ourselves and other people. It can show us the best routes away from danger, and toward our natural spiritual gifts.

HEAD
logic and
reason

HEART
emotions
and dreams

The strategy board is built on the familiar concepts of "head" and "heart" – "head" for logic and reason, and "heart" for emotions and dreams – plus "gut," as in "gut reaction," for instinct and intuition.

GUT
instinct and
intuition

Each of us has just one of these three as our primary influence, guiding us through the complexity of the day: we are head types, or heart types, or gut types.

 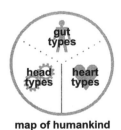

map of the individual　　　　**map of humankind**

As well as the primary influence, some – but not all – have another of the three as an ever-present secondary influence. This moves "home base" on the strategy board from the center of a "zone" over toward that secondary influence – creating a pattern of nine "home bases": the pattern of the nine types. Each home base or "sector" has its own distinctive strategy for approaching the world.

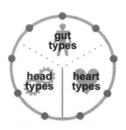

We also change – across the years or just through the day – making moves across the board, often following well-trodden paths. But the most important journey of all is to be made within the home base sector – from the "corrupt" form of the type to its "redeemed" form, from the fallen-ness of the type to its natural spiritual gifts and its unique and vital contribution to the whole body of Christ.

Part 1

Three Zones
and Nine Sectors

Three resources

HEAD
logic and
reason

HEART
emotions
and dreams

To follow the head or to follow the heart? So often we find this conflict in our inner life: logic and reason pull one way, emotions and dreams another. So often a decision has to be made: to follow the head or to follow the heart?

There may be time to contemplate the options – or the time for a decision may be now. In the moment of decision, either head or heart may take priority – or both may be eclipsed by another influence – an almost physical response – the one we call instinct or intuition, or the feeling in our gut or in our bones.

GUT
instinct and
intuition

These three form the foundation of all that follows: in the inner life, both the "head" for logic and reason, and the "heart" for emotions and visions and dreams; and then the "gut," as in "gut reaction," for instinct and intuition, and a more direct and immediate engagement with the world around.

It is in the inner life of the head that we assess and consider the world around. The head is the home of objectivity, logic, analysis, and detailed future plans. In the head we consider questions of meaning – and of how we ought to live. The head is the home of observation and calculation, and of language, rationality, and thought.

It is in the inner life of the heart that we feel emotions – about the world around us, and about our lives in that world. It is from the heart that we reach out to others and long for others to reach out to us. The heart is the home of emotions, memories, images, visions, and dreams. Emotional engagement is the project of the heart.

And then there is this third option: to follow our instinct or intuition, our gut reaction, or the feeling in our bones. The gut – this third "center of intelligence" – operates right in the present moment. It is open and unselfconscious: immediate, practical, and direct.

We all have all three of these "resources," these three "centers of intelligence" – head and heart and gut. All three have value, all three can have virtue – indeed, all three can be spiritual.

It is the distinctive interaction of these three in each one of us that makes us who we are as we begin to engage with the world.

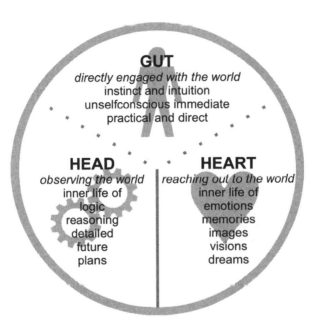

GUT
directly engaged with the world
instinct and intuition
unselfconscious immediate
practical and direct

HEAD
observing the world
inner life of
logic
reasoning
detailed
future
plans

HEART
reaching out to the world
inner life of
emotions
memories
images
visions
dreams

Meeting the world

The world in which we live is an amazing place. In all its created beauty, and in its human population in particular, it is endlessly surprising and inspiring, constantly feeding us new ideas, new images, and new experiences. It can be exciting, thrilling, and rewarding; it can also be hostile, dangerous, and cruel. It is continuously new.

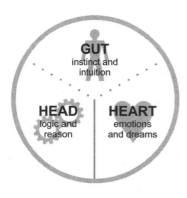

We meet this world, and head and heart and gut respond.

Follow the head, or follow the heart, or follow the gut? There is rarely time to consider – so for each of us just one of the three takes the lead as our primary guide through the complexity of the day. We may change over time, but for today, at least, we are head types, and heart types, and gut types.

In each new situation, the response of the head – and therefore of the head types – is to remain objective and logical: to observe and assess, and then decide.

The response of the heart – and therefore of the heart types – is a longing to have some kind of emotionally meaningful interaction with the people around.

The gut response – and therefore the response of the gut types – is to see the situation in practical or functional terms: to engage in an unselfconscious and open manner, and see how it goes.

To see the process in action, imagine this example of meeting the world: you walk into a room full of people you do not know. How do you respond?

HEAD
logic and
reason

If your head response is dominant, you feel your thought processes going into overdrive, trying by a grand feat of mental calculation to work it all out: to work out what is going on and therefore what to do. You can almost hear the cogs turning in the brain. The head wants to observe and assess and decide before engaging with the new situation.

HEART
emotions
and dreams

In contrast, if your heart response is dominant, you feel your heart beating strong and longing to reach out to the hearts of every other person in the room, to affect them emotionally, to make them love you, straight away. You want to put your heart on your sleeve, and you want everyone there to do likewise. You want to be emotionally close to those people, as soon as possible and for ever.

GUT
instinct and
intuition

And if your gut response is dominant, your response is all about practical and direct engagement with the situation as you find it. You trust your gut instincts and you go with your intuition. You offer to others – and you expect in return – the practical simplicity of "what you see is what you get". Your approach is direct and open, very present tense, very here and now.

Each of us has just one of these three as our primary influence – we are head types, or heart types, or gut types – so our three-zone map of the individual becomes a three-zone map of humankind.

map of the individual

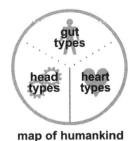

map of humankind

Some people have one of the three resources as their primary influence and keep the other two resources equally in reserve. In this case we say that the individual's "home base" is in the center of one of the three zones – indicated by points THREE and SIX and NINE on the diagram.

Other people still have one of the three resources as their primary influence – but also have one of the other two resources as an ever-present secondary influence, significantly stronger than the third and final resource. In this case we say that the individual's "home base" is not in the center of their "home zone," but off-center, over toward that ever-present secondary influence – indicated by points EIGHT and ONE, and TWO and FOUR, and FIVE and SEVEN on the diagram.

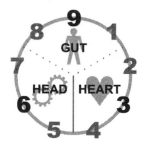

EIGHT, for example, would be the gut type with an ever-present secondary head influence stronger than the heart influence; while ONE would be the gut type with an ever-present secondary heart influence stronger than the head influence; and NINE is the gut type with head and heart equally accessible and available, both kept equally in reserve. The same logic applies for heart types TWO and FOUR and for head types FIVE and SEVEN, each having a primary and secondary influence.

Each of the nine "sectors" on the diagram represents a different, distinctive interaction of head and heart and gut – and so a different, distinctive approach to the challenge of how to meet the day and engage with the world.

Nine strategies

In order to face the countless choices of the day, we each adopt a strategy: a single dependable "first response" for immediate use in each new situation. Our usual strategy emerges over time from our usual interaction of head and heart and gut: it is the strategy of our "home base" on what now becomes "the strategy board."

Gut zone – three strategies

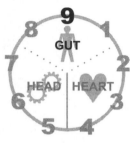

GUT (NINE)
"keep it simple"

The main "gut reaction" strategy for approaching the day could be described in three words: "keep it simple." It focuses on the present tense, on the here and now. It avoids any unnecessary, complicating over-involvement of the head or the heart, and simply deals with each situation as it comes around. As a general strategy for meeting the world, "keep it simple" is on the strategy board as strategy number NINE.

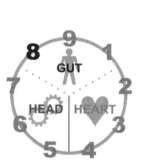

GUT + head (EIGHT)
"test people out"

Stay in the gut zone but add some head influence and we have an approach to the day that still wants to engage directly with people and the world around, but as a secondary priority wants to analyze what is going on, for future reference. Engaging directly, it conducts experiments, and watches for the response. As a general strategy for meeting the world, "test people out" is on the strategy board as strategy number EIGHT.

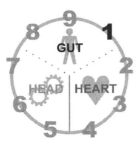

GUT + heart (ONE)
"be on your best behavior"

At the other end of the gut zone, we have an approach to the day that still wants to engage directly, but which cares less – in the immediate moment – about learning for the future, and more about the immediate emotional consequences of the engagement for self and for others. This concern is the origin of the all-purpose strategy "be on your best behavior" – on the board at ONE, the heart end of the gut zone.

Heart zone – three strategies

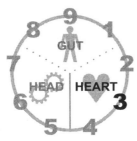

HEART (THREE)
"achieve and lead"

For the heart types, the emotional realm is not secondary but primary: heart types long to reach out to the hearts of others. One way to do this is to achieve something that other hearts will respect: this may involve doing something significant on everybody's behalf, or binding a group together as a leader. As a general strategy for meeting the world, "achieve and lead" is on the strategy board in the center of the heart zone at THREE.

HEART + gut (TWO)
"give and care"

Stay in the heart zone, but add a strong gut influence, and the result is a longing for emotional engagement that also wants to be practical and direct. Giving and caring are driven primarily from the heart zone, but are also practical and direct: as a general strategy for meeting the world, "give and care" is on the board at TWO.

HEART + head (FOUR)
"be true to yourself"

Stay in the heart zone, but add a strong head influence, and the individual will ponder at length how best to organize the heart's interaction with the world. Very aware of the inner life of head and heart – especially heart – the resolution made in sector FOUR is to approach each day and each situation with this one strategy: "be true to yourself."

Head zone – three strategies

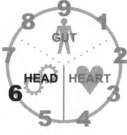

HEAD (SIX)
"stick with
what you know"

Finally, in the head zone, the main head strategy for approaching the day and meeting the world is "stick with what you know." This straightforward head strategy is in the center of the head zone at SIX.

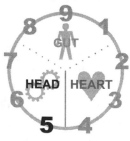

HEAD + heart (FIVE)
"think it through first"

In the head zone but with influence from the heart, there is a concern about all the consequences of any decision to act. In sector FIVE, the head strategy with heart influence is "think it through first."

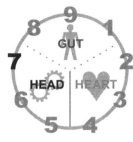

And finally, in the head zone but with a gut influence, there is a calculated determination to be practical and direct, and – it is only logical – to continue being practical and direct, whatever may happen. "Stay positive, come what may" is a head decision – the head strategy with gut influence, at SEVEN.

HEAD + gut (SEVEN)
"stay positive
come what may"

The Nine Strategies
from head and heart and gut reactions

Nine types

Your usual strategy determines your approach to anything new – so over time it comes to define the whole of the way in which you interact with the world around. It affects how you see the rest of the world. It affects how other people see you. If affects your patterns of thinking and feeling and doing. It even determines which temptations you face and which virtues and spiritual gifts are most easily within your reach. Identifying your usual strategy can help you to understand yourself and the spiritual journey in which you are engaged.

All of this is within just one sector of the board. The nine sectors repeat the process for each of the nine strategies – for each of the nine "types." This means that the strategy board can also help you to understand other people – their weaknesses, their potential gifts, and the struggles and the spiritual journeys in which they are engaged – making it so much easier to respect them, work alongside them, engage with them, and value their gifts.

We shall see in due course that the strategies themselves are both morally neutral and practically neutral – none is any better or any worse than any other, morally or practically. Different consequences flow from each strategy depending on whether it is used in a "corrupt," self-interested, and self-centered way, or in a more "redeemed," generous, and godly way. The strategy itself is neutral.

In our complex human lives, each of the types overlaps with the adjacent types on the board, and people also make moves across the board – often following specific well-trodden paths from sector to sector. Most people have at least some access to all nine sectors – but only one of the nine is home base: only one strategy is their usual strategy for engaging with the world through the complexity of the day.

The nine pen portraits that follow are "single strategy" caricatures – but prepare to recognize distinctive aspects of yourself and other people nonetheless.

The Nine Types
from the nine strategies

Gut types – introduction

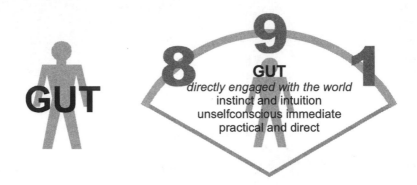

GUT
directly engaged with the world
instinct and intuition
unselfconscious immediate
practical and direct

It is in our human flesh and blood that we live out our lives. It is in the body, the physical human form, that we recognize and meet each other, communicate with one another, and organize all of our human endeavors. It is in our incarnation – our embodiment – that we come to birth and live out the fullness of our lives. Ultimately every meeting of hearts and minds is mediated through our human flesh and blood: our five senses, and our words and deeds.

For all of us, whichever zone may take the lead now in our engagement with the world, the "body" zone – the gut zone – came first.

Evolutionary history places the body first – and the Scriptures in Genesis place the body first. In Genesis, God takes dust from the earth, and from the dust forms humankind: life and spirit are breathed into us to give us mind and heart but it begins with the body, our physical human form. In the New Testament the dignity and beauty of our created human form are affirmed most profoundly as God comes among us in Jesus Christ: from birth through childhood and adulthood and to the cross, God in Christ lives and dies the incarnate, embodied human life.

It is the gut types, the body types, EIGHT and NINE and ONE, who feel most at home in their human flesh and blood, most naturally a part of the rest of creation, most easily at home in the physical world, content to be created a part of it.

Meeting some awesome natural phenomenon of the physical world – ocean or mountain or canyon or starry sky – head types will not feel that they have processed the experience satisfactorily until they have described it in words. Heart types will not feel that they have processed the experience satisfactorily until they have linked it to a collection of emotions. Gut types just connect to it directly and know that they belong, part of creation along with all of creation – incarnate, embodied, directly engaged.

As for a natural phenomenon, so also for a room full of strangers. Head types fill with thoughts; heart types fill with emotions; gut types just know that they are a part of it, engage directly, trust their instincts, and go with their intuition.

If the gut response is dominant, then what you feel as you encounter the world is more likely to be in the pit of your stomach and in your veins than in your head or in your heart. Your action will be more spontaneous than calculated. Your approach is immediate, practical, open, and direct. Your strategy places you in gear straight away, engaging with the world exactly as you find it, here and now, in the present tense, getting on, and moving on.

These are the gut types.

EIGHT

GUT + head (EIGHT)
"test people out"

There is a secondary head influence in gut type EIGHT. In their direct engagement with the world, head-influenced EIGHTs want to work out what is going on – and they do so by engaging directly with their situation: EIGHTs try things out, and observe the results.

EIGHTs are constantly performing experiments on the world around. They might kick or poke some material in order to discover its properties. And in the same way they might kick or poke other people in order to discover their properties – usually metaphorically rather than literally.

The strategy of EIGHTs, encountering the world, is to test people out.

Following this practical strategy, EIGHTs can come across as confrontational and argumentative. They don't mean it. This is just how they do their research into how the world works. This is how EIGHTs interact with it all. EIGHTs can regard a good argument as a form of intimacy: "clearing the air" by "getting it all out in the open" genuinely helps EIGHTs, and makes them feel close to the people who were with them at the time.

EIGHTs will not respect your position if it changes the moment they apply a little pressure. To work in a way that works for EIGHTs, you have to learn to "give as good as you get" – and they'll take it. You may find it tough, but they will not hold it against you. They want you to stand up to them: that is how they begin to understand you, as they do their research into how the world works. EIGHTs will kick all your boundaries – and to win their respect, you have to hold the line.

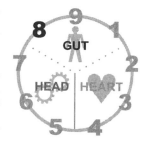

EIGHTs actually test out everything around them – people, systems, networks, authority structures, and the boundaries of their own potential in the world. They kick against the boundaries, and soon learn to detect very quickly where power and weakness lie – in any system or structure or network, or in any individual. As a consequence, EIGHTs can be incredible intuitive problem solvers. In complex situations, they are often the first to realize what is really going on – and they know exactly where to direct their attention to exercise an influence, gaining maximum effect for minimum intervention.

At the corrupt extreme, this makes EIGHTs terrifyingly effective bullies – bullying can be a completely effortless pastime for corrupt EIGHTs. At the opposite extreme, the more redeemed of EIGHTs can be tirelessly efficient fighters for justice: they can identify the processes and effects of power structures of all kinds – economic, educational, democratic, social – at the global and at the immediately local level – and so unmask and challenge the powerful in defense the weak. Repeatedly EIGHTs become both fighters and protectors – dealing in the currency of weakness and of power.

Testing people out is one practical strategy for interacting with our complex and ambiguous world – but it is not the whole picture of the person behind the strategy. We all have heart as well as head and gut: EIGHT is "thick skinned," but still protecting the heart within. EIGHT can be "hard shell, soft center." Male EIGHTs can be "macho boys" – macho man on the outside, little boy on the inside. And by the same contrast, EIGHT is also a natural home for strong women: with their external strategy EIGHT, strong women can take on a male-dominated world and keep up or get ahead – with the heart protected within.

A cartoon animal for EIGHT is the bull – capable of deliberate aggression and a serious fight. But like a bull in a china shop – innocently making its way from the door to the till like everyone else – EIGHT is often completely unaware of the chaos in its wake. And despite all that bulk and strength, in those big soft eyes you may just catch a glimpse of a gentle spirit within, and perhaps the basic compassionate longing to use strength to protect.

EIGHT can also be the tiger – knowledgeable, fast moving, effortlessly powerful.

And sometimes EIGHT is the tiger cub. In pairs or in groups, tiger cubs will play-fight, gnawing at each other playfully – in the way they will later kill their prey. Playfully chasing and wrestling, every so often they will nip or claw each other slightly harder than intended, and suddenly there is tension: a hiss, aggression, a stand-off. At that moment, are they playing or fighting? For a moment, neither is quite sure. That is how it can be relating to an EIGHT. Even in the long term, years into the relationship, you may find yourself engaged in some conversation where you are not quite sure whether your companion is playing or fighting – laughing with you or mocking you. That can be EIGHT, still testing you out.

A national stereotype for EIGHT would be southern European men – who can have a stand-up argument in a restaurant and then sit down and carry on as if nothing had happened.

In the Bible we see the strong women – Miriam, Deborah, Hannah – and strong men with vulnerabilities – Samson, Saul – and the harp-playing warrior, lover of Jonathan yet slayer of tens of thousands, the boy king David.

The temptations of EIGHT are all power issues: arrogance and revenge and retaliation. And so are the potential gifts: a keen sense of justice, and support for the powerless or weak.

EIGHTs on the journey from corruption to redemption will be realizing that other people deserve respect even when they do not choose to rise to the fight: that other people have other gifts which are expressed in different ways. They will also be finding the ability to show mercy, discovering the protector instinct, and getting in touch with the child within.

test people out
8 JUSTICE
fighter protector
southern european men
testing boundaries
tiger cub bull
David *bullying*
arrogance
revenge

EIGHT (GUT + head)
Strategy: test people out
Fighters and protectors, kicking against the boundaries, sensing where power lies; hard shell, soft center; strong women; macho boys. Corrupt EIGHTs can be bullies destroying every rival. Redeemed EIGHTs can be protectors of the weak and fighters for justice.
Temptations: arrogance, revenge, retaliation
Gifts: justice, support for the powerless or weak
Animals: bull, tiger, tiger cub
National stereotype: southern European men
In the Bible: Miriam, Deborah, Hannah, Samson, Saul, David
Paths to redemption: Respect others. Find the ability to show mercy. Discover the protector instinct. Get in touch with the child within.

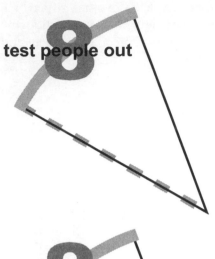

A graphic serves as a quick reference for the key features of each sector.

The shape indicates the sector's location on the board. It is labeled with its number – which is purely for reference – and its strategy – which determines every other feature of the sector.

The temptations are placed "down at the sharp end of the wedge" – in Roman type. The gifts are placed out at the "broad, open" end of the wedge – in **CAPITALS**.

Finally we add a selection of other characteristics and mnemonics for the sector in regular type –

and complement the diagram with a short description including key features and mnemonics (right).

test people out
JUSTICE
fighter protector
southern european men
testing boundaries
tiger cub bull
David
bullying
arrogance
revenge

EIGHT (GUT + head)
Strategy: test people out
Fighters and protectors, kicking against the boundaries, sensing where power lies; hard shell, soft center; strong women; macho boys. Corrupt EIGHTs can be bullies destroying every rival. Redeemed EIGHTs can be protectors of the weak and fighters for justice.
Temptations: arrogance, revenge, retaliation
Gifts: justice, support for the powerless or weak
Animals: bull, tiger, tiger cub
National stereotype: southern European men
In the Bible: Miriam, Deborah, Hannah, Samson, Saul, David
Paths to redemption: Respect others. Find the ability to show mercy. Discover the protector instinct. Get in touch with the child within.

NINE

GUT (NINE)
"keep it simple"

In the center of the gut zone, made from the dust of the earth, NINEs are completely at home in the physical world. They engage directly and straightforwardly with the rest of creation, including the rest of humankind. They live in the present tense, in the here and now. They avoid any unnecessary, complicating over-involvement of the head or the heart. NINEs have about them the innocence of Eden: a restful, calming presence, an attractive simplicity, and an unflappable inertia.

The strategy of NINEs is to keep it simple: to deal with each new situation as it comes around, in whatever practical manner seems most appropriate at the time.

A cartoon animal for NINE is the dolphin. Dolphins and whales spend three quarters of their time playing and just one quarter feeding. When you see them dipping and diving and jumping, often in groups, they really are just playing and having fun, for no reason except that that is what they do. That is the innocence of Eden of NINE.

Another cartoon animal for NINE is the elephant. Elephants are always surrounded by happy people. That is NINE: it is easy to like a NINE; everybody loves a NINE. And then you can push and kick a stationary elephant all you like, but you cannot move it. It will not move. That is also NINE. Until – the elephant decides for itself that it wants to move – decides, indeed, that it is going to perform some major task, such as moving a great tree trunk from one place to another. The elephant then moves, determinedly, unstoppably, calmly, single-mindedly, and it really is best not to get in the way, and it really is pointless to try to stop it or to shout out alternative methods or routes. The elephant is about its task and the task will be done. That is the unflappable inertia of NINE.

NINEs accept others without prejudice. Modern, easy-going friendships are very NINE. NINEs can often come and go without being much noticed, and do not mind being invisible. They do not expect to stand out, and tend to be surprised by attention. NINEs are honest and uncomplicated: they have no hidden motives. In meeting the world on its own terms, exactly as it is, they somehow combine a gentle cynicism with an easy trust.

NINEs' instinct for simplicity means they can sense immediately when something has been made unnecessarily complicated. This inbuilt detector of unnecessary complications helps to make NINEs into reconcilers: they know straight away when the point at stake is not worth the cost of the argument, and they aim instead for the simplicity of peace.

Keeping things simple, NINEs often avoid making decisions, and would not bother having an opinion on something unless they actually needed one. This is often a good thing in our divided and opinionated world – again it makes NINEs into natural peacemakers and reconcilers. It also means that NINEs can find themselves swept along, and then be annoyed with themselves for having been. They can also find themselves knowing better what they do not want than what they do want. All of this comes from NINE's primary reliance on instinct and intuition – avoiding the complexity of involving head or heart until absolutely necessary.

The national stereotype for easy-going NINE is Africa – or think of African culture in the Caribbean. Westerners have watches; Africans have time.

In the Bible, Jonah is NINE. God said go this way, but Jonah did not fancy the task, so went the other way instead. In the great storm at sea, only Jonah was fast asleep "in the inner part of the ship": NINEs can sleep anywhere, any time. It took a whale to get Jonah to the right place, where he finally set about the assigned task with simple clarity and consequent success – which distressed him greatly, as it disturbed the simple worldview in which Ninevites are evil and can be safely condemned or ignored. At the end of the book, Jonah sits glumly outside the city, and God tries in vain to budge his mood. That is also NINE.

The simplicity of NINE redeemed can be steadfast and goal-oriented, and of all the types, it is peaceful, open, and direct NINEs who are most able to speak hard truths calmly.

The temptations of NINE are idleness, complacency, and fatalism; also narcosis – from peacefulness through idleness and into oblivion. And gut type NINE's aggression, when it shows, is "passive aggressive" – stubborn, or obstinate, or sulking without remorse: the elephant can stand in your way, and no kick or shout will move it. That is "passive aggressive," and that can be NINE.

On the path from corruption to redemption, stationary NINEs begin to move – discovering their gifts, their energy, their self-worth, and their inner drive, overcoming their cynicism or dismissiveness in order to choose priorities – well – and then act.

NINE (GUT)

Strategy: keep it simple

Restful, calming presence; an attractive simplicity; inertia; the meek. Corrupt NINEs can be stubborn, obstinate, complacent, neglectful, idle, and fatalistic. Redeemed NINEs can be steadfast, goal-oriented, and peacemakers able to speak hard truths calmly.

Temptations: idleness, complacency, fatalism; narcosis

Gifts: peace, reconciliation, humility

Animals: dolphin, elephant

National stereotype: Africa

In the Bible: Jonah

Paths to redemption: Find gifts and energy, self-worth and inner drive. Overcome cynicism. Choose priorities – well – and then act. Develop mind and heart.

ONE

GUT + heart (ONE)
"be on your best behavior"

Gut types engage directly with the world – so any judgment on what they do, whether criticism or praise, feels like a judgment on who they are.

EIGHTs and NINEs just shrug this off – "who cares what other people think" – but ONEs are the gut types with a secondary heart influence. ONEs do care what other people think.

And being intuitive gut types, ONEs sense every judgment of approval or disapproval from others whether it is spoken or not. Those judgments then echo around inside, where they become like an ever-present internal critic – a powerful gut-level conscience – passing judgment on every thought, feeling, and action.

Determined to attract more approval and to avoid all disapproval, the strategy of ONEs is to be "on their best behavior" – to be "good" by the standards of the powerful conscience within. They then expect the same of others: on the small scale, on the universal scale, and everywhere in between, ONEs long for everything to be done well. ONEs become perfectionists and idealists.

The perfectionist's eye for detail makes ONEs into great engineers, accountants, judges, and lawyers. Wherever it is important that something is done with precision – design issues, safety issues, legal or financial matters, organizing a major project – ONEs are indispensable, being both thorough and efficient, including whatever is necessary, and excluding whatever is not.

The parable of the lost sheep is the parable for ONEs: everyone else is really happy that there are ninety-nine sheep in the sheepfold – ninety-nine is plenty, and the day's work is done – but while everyone else relaxes at the end of the day, ONE is out on the hills alone in the dark and the rain looking for the one lost sheep. ONEs are the ones who

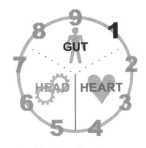

will always make sure that no detail – and no individual – is ever overlooked, and they will carry on, patient and steadfast, until their work is done. ONEs have limitless energy in the service of idealism and fairness to all (Matthew 18:12-14; Luke 15:3-7).

The potential gifts of ONE include patience and serenity. ONEs can take on a complex task and see it through to completion: they can see the end of a defined task from its beginning, and all the stages in between, and they can attend to the task – to put everything exactly right – with perfect patience, ticking off the stages as they go, even under huge pressure or in the midst of a crisis. And in a serious crisis or emergency, efficient and thorough ONEs can remain calm and composed: they remain "on their best behavior," and assess what actually needs to be done, and then efficiently attend to it; their moment has come to be the good boy scout or the good girl guide. ONEs can keep their heads when all around are losing theirs: even in complex stressful times, ONEs will work on and on toward completion and perfection.

The danger for ONEs is that this visionary idealism can become judgmental and unforgiving toward all that is less than perfect – in others, and in themselves. Being judgmental and unforgiving toward others, they can be self-righteous and hypocritical on the outside. Being judgmental and unforgiving toward themselves, they can at the same time be suffering low self-esteem on the inside.

These are clear and unambiguous dangers: the temptation that creeps up on ONE far more subtly is anger. ONE's anger begins as "righteous anger" at the injustice and imperfection of the world. It is compounded by frustration at the imperfections in self and others. It can build into a continuous, rumbling, low-level,

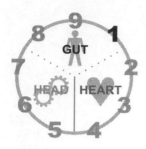

frustrated, "free floating" anger – just waiting for something on which to alight. The slightest incidence of real or perceived unfairness then sparks the fuse, and the anger of ONE ignites – and is slow to calm. Being patronized is an unfairness that ONEs cannot bear, and it is guaranteed to ignite a ONE on a short fuse. As ONE tries to maintain the "good" exterior, the anger is often repressed, and suffered far more by ONE than by others.

The cartoon animals for ONE are the terrier – noisily yapping and snapping away – and the ant and bee – busy, busy, busy about their task.

The national stereotype for ONE would be Switzerland – for the clocks, and the watches, and the banks, and those efficient little army knives.

In the Bible, Paul is ONE. It is important to Paul to explain, with clarity and completeness, exactly how the crucifixion makes salvation possible, how grace and law interact or oppose each other, how one era ends and a new era begins – exactly how God does God's work of salvation. This is all very ONE: others would be less concerned to give such a detailed, almost mechanical, account. But it is in precisely these details that Paul finds his limitless energy for the proclamation of the gospel, and his dogged determination to see the Gentiles included in God's new work in Christ – when others are disinterested or even opposed. The vast majority of Christian people today came to hear the good news of salvation in Jesus Christ by way of Paul's ONE: his clarity about God's work of salvation, and his long and principled stand for the inclusion of the Gentiles without their needing to submit to the Hebrew law. It is no surprise that Luther, also ONE, found his inspiration in Paul: reforming zeal is ONE.

ONEs set out on the path from corruption to redemption by relaxing a little – by letting the spring unwind. In practical terms, for ONEs, this usually means deliberately programming some recreation and leisure into their detailed, busy schedules. ONEs on the path to redemption will learn to learn from others, who think in a different way, and learn to accommodate the imperfections of themselves and the rest of the world – learn that it is OK to be human. A major milestone for ONEs is the day they learn with confidence to challenge the nagging internal critic: to stand up to it and assert their freedom to choose otherwise – even to do something reckless or pointless, just for fun, just to be fully alive.

ONE (GUT + heart)
Strategy: be on your best behavior
Idealists and perfectionists, good boys and girls. Corrupt ONEs can be judgmental, hypocritical, unforgiving. Redeemed ONEs can be hard working, honest and reliable, with limitless energy in the service of idealism and fairness to all.
Temptation: anger
Gifts: patience, idealism, fairness for all, serenity
Animals: terrier; ant and bee
National stereotype: Switzerland
In the Bible: Saint Paul
Paths to redemption: Program in some recreation and leisure. Learn to learn from others, who think in a different way. Accept the imperfection in the world: "it's OK to be human." Challenge the nagging internal critic.

Gut types – review

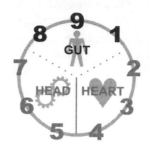

GUT
directly engaged with the world
instinct and intuition
unselfconscious immediate
practical and direct

It has been said that EIGHTs just love to be bad – always kicking against the boundaries of what is possible. And ONEs just love to be good – always on their best behavior. What they have in common with each other – and with peaceful NINEs as well – is that they engage very directly with the world around them. Further down the board, in the heart zone and the head zone, there are detached, self-conscious calculations and meditations concerning the world around. Here in the gut zone, there is no detached calculation, no complex future scheme, and no deep echo from the long-forgotten past. What you see is what you get – and it is unselfconscious, immediate, practical, and direct.

The gut types redeemed share a passion for direct engagement with the world to make the world a better place. The argument between EIGHT and ONE is whether the best means is revolution or reform. The instinct of "best behavior" ONE is reform – to work within the system to change the system. The instinct of EIGHT is revolution – to kick down the established power structures – to be bad in the established order's terms. EIGHT may persuade ONE that the true service of all that is right and good is the "efficient" removal of the existing regime. Or ONE may persuade EIGHT that the realities of power and weakness are such that reform is possible, and revolution is not. NINE may "hold the balance of power" and build a gut types consensus around NINE's own instincts for long-term peace and reconciliation. Whether by revolution or reform or just long-term hard work, the gut types redeemed will share a passion to make the world a better place.

Reaching that redeemed place – for all three gut types – does involve getting in touch with head and heart. Confrontational EIGHTs – on the head side – need to find their heart. Impulsive and judgmental ONEs – on the heart side – need to do some thinking and some learning. NINEs need to find some access to both head and heart in order to find their wholeness and their energy. But the best gifts of all three remain right there in their own home sectors: EIGHTs as natural protectors and fighters for justice; NINEs as natural reconcilers and peacemakers; and ONEs as the ones who will ensure that every single person is given the full dignity of being a child of God, without any being overlooked – because anything less is imperfect and incomplete.

The Gut Types

keep it simple

PEACE
innocence of Eden
easy-going
elephant
dolphin
Jonah
Africa

test people out
JUSTICE
fighter protector
southern european men
testing boundaries
tiger cub   bull
David
revenge   arrogance   bullying   stubbornness   idleness   fatalistic   anger

be on your
best behaviour
FAIRNESS FOR ALL
PATIENCE
IDEALISM   SERENITY
perfectionism   terrier
ant and bee
Switzerland
Saint Paul

Overview – corruption and redemption

We can talk about redemption in all three tenses: past, present, and future.

In the past tense, we were redeemed from corruption when the saving work of Christ first took effect in our lives.

In the future tense, we shall be redeemed from corruption when sin and corruption are finally left behind forever in the glory of eternity.

And in the present tense, we are even now engaged in the journey from corruption to redemption – as we seek daily, by God's grace, to become less like the worst of what we have been, and more like the best of what God wants us to be.

We are still on that journey from corruption to redemption – with elements of both in our lives. God has not finished with any of us yet.

As we examine the "corrupt" and "redeemed" consequences of each of the nine strategies, it is important to remember that the strategies themselves are all neutral. It is all too easy to classify different types as good or bad – morally or practically. This might happen if some of the images in the descriptions happen to resonate more clearly than others on a first read through. And it might happen because of the particular people you happen to know – each one having a home base on the board, but each one at a different stage on their journey toward redemption.

For each of the nine types, the corrupt form emerges when the strategy is applied in a self-directed, self-centered, self-obsessed manner – the practice of humankind fallen, a corruption of what God intended us to be. The description of each type's redeemed form is a description of what the same strategy could produce when exercised in harmony with God's good will for humankind. The Christian calling is not to move across the board, from one type to another, but to move within the home base sector, from the corrupt form of the type to its redeemed form, from the fallen-ness of the type to its natural spiritual gifts and its unique and vital contribution to the whole body of Christ. The Christian calling is to be fully alive in God as the redeemed form of who we already are.

Heart types – introduction

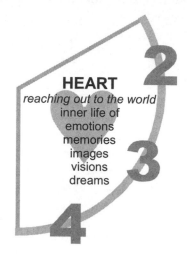

HEART
reaching out to the world
inner life of
emotions
memories
images
visions
dreams

So far we have encountered the gut types, who engage with the present directly as they find it – indeed, they feel very much a part of it.

Heart types, in contrast, work with a clear distinction between the self and the outside world. For heart types, life is lived very consciously leaning across a boundary between what is within – the "self" – and what is outside – everything and everybody else. There is a longing to reach out across that boundary, to influence, to engage – and a clear, almost calculated awareness that that is what is being done.

Inevitably, the heart types assume – wrongly – that everyone else engages with the world in the same way, self-consciously leaning across a boundary between what is within and what is outside.

As they reach out across that boundary, the goal of all three heart types is to stir up love.

In its redeemed form, this goal is a truly beautiful and selfless thing – to stir up love all around, for its own sake and for the sake of all created things: this is the gift of the heart. If some particular person chooses not to be stirred up, the redeemed heart type just shrugs and moves on, allowing that person their own space and time, their own pilgrimage, to find their ability to love.

Wholly corrupted, made selfish and self-directed, the heart type begins to demand love – as if such a thing were possible. It can become a desperate imposition on others around.

It is a healthy heart, with a sense of its own identity, which can be truly generous to others – rather than dependent and demanding. To keep a healthy heart, it is good for heart types to invest at least some resources in nurturing, strengthening, and cherishing the heart of the self – rather than investing everything they have in the intricate details of their relationships with others. Either way, for the heart types, it is always about reaching out to the world from the inner life of the heart – the inner life of emotions and memories, of images and visions and dreams.

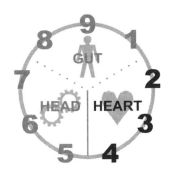

TWO

HEART + gut (TWO)
"give and care"

TWO is a heart-gut combination – the heart, taking the lead, reaching out in the service of love, and the added gut influence giving an instinct for direct action in the world. Direct action in the service of love is giving and caring. The strategy of TWOs – in the service of the heart – is to give and to care.

TWOs have powerful talents for their task – beginning with a remarkable heart-and-gut intuition for where needs lie: TWOs can sense a hidden need at a hundred paces, and they can read you like a book. From the same heart and gut combination comes a direct engagement with individuals: TWO's natural domain is the one-to-one relationship. TWOs have a memory for detail which is like a vast filing cabinet storing information on each of their one-to-one relationships in turn: when you meet only for the second time, TWO will remember every detail of your interaction the time before – how you take your coffee, where your family lives, the names of the friends you were seeing that evening. And finally there is TWO's charm: the heart and gut combination means that TWO connects with you immediately, and you are drawn in straight away.

This is a powerful set of talents – insight, one-to-one engagement, memory for detail, and charm. On the telephone or at the enquiry desk TWOs are totally attentive and could not be more helpful. As a company representative a TWO could convince you that the entire organization is committed exclusively to your welfare. TWOs could sell you anything and make you feel good about buying it.

As for the virtue of giving and caring to stir up love, it all depends on whether TWO is stirring up love for the sake of love – a high

Christian calling – or stirring up love for the sake of TWO – fishing for compliments, giving in order to receive. Either way, TWO has a powerful set of talents to hand.

Turned to self-interest, the strategy and talents of TWO can be smothering, demanding, intrusive, intimidating – even manipulative. This TWO wants to keep control of every aspect of the relationship – and ultimately control you. It can be patronizing and possessive.

Turned to the interests of love alone, giving and caring TWO becomes the perfect biblical model of selfless, generous, unconditional love. TWO redeemed will care for your nourishment, education, welfare, even self-belief – would stand by you in any suffering or pain or conflict, whatever its cause – would forgive anything, give their last ounce of energy, come running in a crisis – and would care like this for friend and stranger alike, for the respectable and for the outcast, and await no reward, not even recognition, not even from the beneficiary. This is the high Christian calling to stir up love for the sake of love alone, to give and care unconditionally for the good of all creation.

Either way, it is through giving and caring to stir up love that TWO finds a role in the world, a way to interact, a strategy.

Mother Teresa is the patron saint of TWOs – of all natural benefactors, givers and helpers.

In the Scriptures, the traditional Mary Magdalene is TWO, washing Jesus' feet with her hair – a simple act of generous and compassionate kindness and care; also Martha, fussing with the serving instead of listening; and supremely Saint John, "the disciple whom Jesus loved," promoting and promoting above all else that we must love one another.

The national stereotype for TWO is the Italian mother: powerful, strong, caring – and demanding.

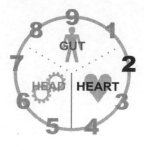

A cartoon animal for TWO is the clucking mother hen, marshalling her brood – or the enthusiastic licking puppy: the affectionate attention is charming at first, but after a while its target may be saying "enough now! Go away!"

The temptation of TWO is pride: "I do all this giving, they all depend on me, I have earned my reward."

The potential gifts of TWO are a genuinely unconditional kindness and generosity.

On the path from corruption to redemption, TWOs come to recognize that their individual high Christian calling is just one small part of God's much wider plan for the good of the whole world: TWO is not alone in an endless task, but a co-worker with God and with others; God has other plans for some of the needs they see – and cares about TWOs as well. "Let go and let God" is good advice for TWOs: it gives TWOs the liberating permission to invest at least some of their resources in nurturing, strengthening, and cherishing themselves, rather than investing everything in others. TWOs can then engage with the hearts of others with generosity, instead of neediness, to the fore. It also makes it possible for TWO to form some healthy, symmetrical "co-worker" relationships, where TWO can both give and receive freely as an equal, perhaps for the first time. Making some space to nurture and refresh the self, balancing action with contemplation, TWOs – natural givers – learn to receive – from God and from others – and move toward their perfect vocation to be agents of God's compassion in the world.

TWO (HEART + gut)
Strategy: give and care
Sensing needs, often reading people like a book. Corrupt TWOs can be
smothering, demanding, manipulative. Redeemed TWOs can be
unconditionally generous, self-giving, nurturing, caring for others' body, mind,
and soul.
Temptations: pride – in the classic sense of self-importance;
possessiveness
Gifts: kindness, generosity
Animal: licking puppy
National stereotype: Italian mother
In the Bible: Saint John, Mary Magdalene, Martha
Paths to redemption: Admit own needs, and attend to them as well as
others'. Let God take care of some needs. Make some symmetrical
relationships.

THREE

HEART (THREE)
"achieve and lead"

THREEs – in the middle of the heart zone – have a particular talent of the heart for working with the complexities of group dynamics. Others may find it difficult or artificial to have to work within a group or as part of a team, but this is where THREEs can thrive: the group is THREE's favored environment. The strategy of heart type THREEs – to stir up love – is to be inspirational in the group: achieving something significant on everybody's behalf, or working to bind the group together.

THREEs inspire friendship and fellowship within a group, and draw people together around shared goals and ideals. THREEs turn a group into a team. The natural team leadership of THREE is not domineering from outside the group, but inspirational from within.

Redeemed THREEs work within the group for the group – not only being the best that THREE can be, for the sake of the group, but also identifying and promoting every other talent and ability in the group, encouraging every other person in their potential and in their gifts. THREE inspires hope: the sense that things are possible, that great things can be achieved. And THREE brings a unique gift of gentleness: redeemed THREE knows just how to draw alongside someone, as an equal on the team, to bring encouragement, or to help make everything all right. Redeemed THREE can indeed be "all heart."

For corrupted THREEs, colleagues become rivals and team-mates become opponents, as the goal in interacting with the group changes from the good of all to the good of the self. Corrupt THREEs' lives are dominated by the conscious desire to impress and to lead – and their skills in group dynamics are undiminished, so they may well succeed. In the process, corrupt THREEs can become viciously competitive, trampling on rivals in order to win the position of the most admired, the most loved. Corrupt THREEs may invest so much energy in creating a desirable public

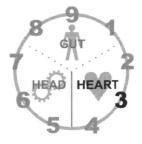

image for themselves that little else remains. As for all the heart types, it is good for THREEs to remember to invest at least some of their resources in nurturing, strengthening, and cherishing the genuine self, rather than investing everything in their public image and its relationship with others.

The national stereotype for group-minded, leading, and achieving THREEs is the mainstream USA. It's in their blood. When the settlers reached the Americas, there were no separate kings or lords or rulers among them – just equal human beings and one vast project. Achieving anything meant working – or competing – within a team of equals. That remains the THREE culture of the mainstream USA to this day.

A cartoon animal for THREE is the eagle – just one of many birds, but soaring higher than the rest, achieving more, visible to all, and inspiring: the best thing on two wings. Another is the chameleon: for better or for worse, for corrupt reasons or redeemed, THREE can change its colors quickly to match each new environment.

There is a lot of team-leader THREE in western politics – corrupt and redeemed: the spirit and practice of democracy promote the idea of leading from within. Count in Bill Clinton, and the public image of New Labour. Inspirational charismatic leadership is THREE. Playing the crowd is THREE. Presenting oneself as the epitome of people's dreams for themselves is THREE. And THREEs love praise – achievement and praise.

The temptation of chameleon THREE is deceit – to say or to do whatever plays well with the audience of the moment. In western politics, call it spin. In the Bible, Jacob is THREE: Jacob the

deceiver, competing with Esau for top ranking – but going on to be the gentle team leader for the nation.

Heart type THREEs are always conscious of their audience. To move along the path from corruption to redemption, it is important for THREEs to spend some time in contemplation – with no audience. The temptation for THREEs is to sit contemplating how they are going to tell everyone what good contemplating they have done, or wondering whether God is impressed yet. Neither counts. On the path from corruption to redemption, THREEs will be examining, with no audience, the false self-image or self-images – and then finding and valuing instead the real self, which is loved by God without any need for a mask or a performance. THREEs can then develop healthy non-competitive relationships, promote and celebrate the gifts of others, and learn from their less successful projects without worrying what the audience may think.

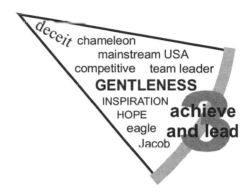

THREE (HEART)
Strategy: achieve and lead
The natural team leader, admired by the group, leading from within, skilled in group dynamics. Corrupt THREEs can be viciously competitive, career addicted, obsessed with image. Redeemed THREEs draw people together, inspire hope, and always want the best for the team.
Temptation: deceit
Gifts: gentleness, inspiration, hope
Animals: chameleon, eagle
National stereotype: mainstream USA
In the Bible: Jacob
Paths to redemption: Contemplation – with no audience. Examine the false self-image: find the real, beautifully created, self. Work with others. Learn humility and gentleness.

FOUR

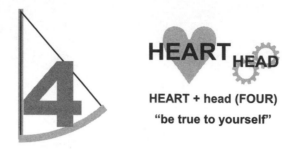

HEART + head (FOUR)
"be true to yourself"

At FOUR we are down at the foot of the diagram – a long way from the gut zone and its direct engagement with the outside world. As a head-heart combination, FOUR is very conscious of the inner life of head and heart, and that inner life – rather than the outside world – is FOUR's natural home. The story of FOUR meeting the world is the story of FOUR's inner life seeking to engage with the outside world from which it feels distant and separate.

FOUR remains a heart type, longing to reach out to the world: it is the heart that takes the lead in FOUR's inner life of head and heart. The challenge for FOURs is how to reach out from the heart within to the world outside.

Head and heart work together on this challenge and come to this resolution: that the best and the only way to relate to the world outside is to remain "true to yourself" – true to the inner self. This is the strategy with which FOUR approaches the world.

Head and heart now get to work on the task of being "true to the inner self" while also – for this is a heart type – reaching out to the world. The key to this task is self-presentation: to create a presentation of the self which is true to the inner self and which also reaches out to the world, bridging that gap between the inner life and the world outside – the world of other people and their separate lives. Dress will be important. Manner will be important. Carefully chosen words will be important. Public choices, like where to go and what to do, will be important. For FOUR, life is a work of art, for which the audience is the world.

But the real story of FOUR is the story of FOUR's inner life. Here, "deep in the heart zone," FOURs experience things intensely. They are in touch with deep emotions – and in touch with the pain of the world. FOURs have often experienced every human emotion by the age of twenty-five. Counselors are taught never to say "I know how you feel" – but from a FOUR it would often be true.

FOURs have a unique talent for appreciating, understanding, and then expressing the things of the heart. Although some will struggle to find their voice – longing to communicate but not finding the means – many FOURs do find their voice in an artistic expression. A classic FOUR type is the artist, producing poetry or music or painting or sculpture which perfectly expresses love and beauty and the profound things of the heart in a way that others can receive but cannot hope to create. For many FOURs, aesthetics are everything, and beauty is what matters.

It has been said that just about everything in the world that is beautiful was created by a FOUR. Much of the rest came from NINEs, who just produce the stuff effortlessly from somewhere in their gut with minimal thought or emotion, much to the envy of the tortured, struggling FOUR.

The inner life of the heart does tend to relive in the present the emotions and visions and dreams of the past. This is most extreme with FOURs, who endlessly reprocess all that they have seen and experienced – everything that has gone before.

Among the gifts of FOUR are profound gifts of the heart: creativity, empathy, profound communication ("communion"), and the ability to convert pain into beauty.

On the down side, FOURs can end up living in the past, or wallowing in self-pity, or withdrawing from the world. Like all the corrupted heart types, corrupt FOURs can end up draining instead of enriching those who meet them. Hypochondria is FOUR. The temptation of FOUR is envy: "why does everyone else have so much easier a life?"

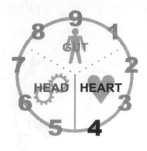

The national stereotype for FOUR is France: in its self-image it stands alone as the most beautiful nation and language and culture, suffering among "vulgar and inferior" neighbors.

A cartoon animal for FOUR is the peacock. That tail serves no practical purpose – but it is incredibly dramatic and beautiful, and that is justification enough. Other natural FOURs are the cooing mourning dove, or the stylish black horse – stylish, dark, and mysterious – or the basset hound with its big sad eyes.

The perfect icon for the vocation of FOUR is the oyster. The oyster turns grit into pearls: it turns pain into beauty.

FOURs in the Bible include Hosea – whose own painful experiences help him to identify with God's sorrow over the sinfulness of Israel – and Isaiah, who gives us the beautiful texts about the suffering servant of God. Jeremiah in Lamentations finds the most beautiful promises of God's faithfulness in the depths of despair, and Shulamith, the initially lonesome lover in Song of Songs, writes beautifully of her passion for her beloved. There is also Joseph, who dreams dreams, understands and interprets dreams, and wears that famously colored coat.

For FOURs, the path from corruption to redemption – from wasted pain to beauty and creativity – involves learning to engage with ordinary non-FOUR people and the wider world – to love in the real world, not reject it as unworthy. This means stilling, or rising above, the endlessly churning emotions, learning to see the beauty in the ordinary, and even learning the art of small talk – demeaning and unworthy though it may at first appear. The peacock discovers that it is possible to have a full and meaningful life as an ordinary farmyard chicken: the fancy tail is a bonus, not the essence; the authentic self is found in ordinary simplicity, not in further striving for yet more difference. To support all of this, FOURs, who are furthest of all from the gut zone, do need to remember three incarnational basics: to take some exercise, get some fresh air, and eat the right food.

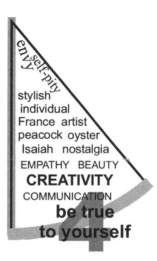

FOUR (HEART + head)
Strategy: be true to yourself
Very aware of the inner life, FOURs have often experienced every human emotion by the age of 25. Corrupt FOURs can wallow in self-pity, live in the past, and withdraw from the world. Redeemed FOURs convert pain into beauty through creativity, sympathy, inspiration, and vision.
Temptations: envy, self-pity
Gifts: creativity, beauty, empathy, communication
Animals: peacock, oyster
National stereotype: France
In the Bible: Isaiah, Hosea, Joseph, Jeremiah
Paths to redemption: Engage with "ordinary" people and the wider world. Learn to love, not reject. See the beauty in the ordinary. Rise above the churning emotions. Take some exercise, get some fresh air, eat the right food.

Heart types – review

HEART
reaching out to the world
inner life of
emotions
memories
images
visions
dreams

There is a saying common in Christian circles – in the form of a piece of advice – that "you must learn to love yourself."

For the practical gut types, and the logical head types, this is a strange saying: it comes close to being logically meaningless, unless translated into practical concepts like attention and care; and then it sounds a little too much like permission to be selfish. It is, in any case, a rather strained derivation from the saying of Jesus which is generally quoted as the relevant source: "love your neighbor as yourself" does not command that attention and care be given to the self, but assumes it to be so; the actual command is not to love the self, but to respect others as equals and give attention and care to them.

But for heart types, this popular saying is actually good advice. Reaching out to others – loving others – comes naturally to heart types. Giving a little attention and care to the self does not, and that is exactly what the heart types need to do. And the self for which the heart types must learn to care is not the carefully constructed actor they present to the world. The heart types have to find the authentic self, the self they can properly present to God in prayer: God who sees everything and still has compassion, God who will not be won over by a show – God who loves anyway, and needs no winning over. Finding that stable place – where the real self meets with God and flourishes – will enrich, and make authentic, all of the heart types' carefully planned interactions between the self and the world around. Heart types need to find that loveable self, and nurture it, strengthen it, cherish it a little – prayerfully, in the presence of God.

As we have considered each of the three heart types in turn, we have seen them reaching out to the world in three distinct ways – deriving as ever from the mix of influences from head and heart and gut. Heart type TWOs – reaching out to the world – use their secondary gut influence to engage with people directly, one-to-one. Heart type THREEs work well with group dynamics, and use that as their primary engagement with the world. The natural home of heart type FOURs – with the added head influence – is the inner life, and FOURs reach out from there to the whole world at once. This creates a pattern, down the right hand side of the board, of relating to the world in different sized "batches": TWOs reach out to other individuals one by one; THREEs relate best to groups; and FOURs reach out from the self within to the whole of the world outside.

More generally, THREE – in the middle of the zone – is "all heart," with the gifts of gentleness and hope. For heart type TWO, it is the added gut influence which first detects needs – by intuition – and then cannot help but rush in to assist: a gut reaction in the service of the heart. And it is the head influence in heart type FOUR which works hard on carefully planned communication and self-presentation: head work in the service of the heart.

Fundamental to all three heart types is the longing to reach out to others – to be emotionally close to the strangers in the room, right away and for ever. Corrupted heart types may have no healthy "self" to offer for that meeting of hearts, and so have to meet on the other person's territory – have to impose. Healthy heart types can offer their own healthy heart's hospitality – they can say "your place or mine" for that meeting of hearts. With a secure and genuine and stable heart of their own, heart types have the opportunity to enter into supportive equal relationships, heart to heart with others – in the service of the heart, in the service of love.

The Heart Types

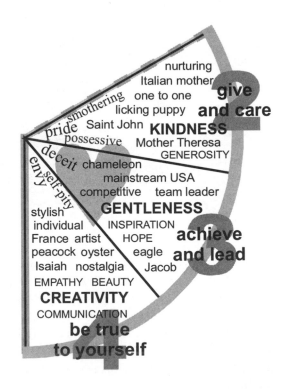

Overview – the symmetry of the board

The strategy board is built on these two familiar aspects of our inner lives: the head, for logic and reason, and the heart, for emotions and dreams. When we have time to consider at length, this is the conflict again and again: to follow the head or to follow the heart. The contrast between the two is the first fundamental dynamic of the strategy board.

Instinct and intuition – the "gut" influence – work in a different way, closer to the point where a decision has to be made. In the complexity of our interactions with the world, head and heart are one kind of influence – internal and self-conscious – and gut is another – unselfconscious, immediate, practical, and direct.

The strategy board has been arranged to highlight this difference. Head and heart go side by side in the lower part of the board, representing the self-conscious inner life, while the gut zone is alone at the top of the board, representing direct engagement with the world.

This arrangement gives the board a heart side – the right hand side of the board – and a head side – the left hand side of the board. Everything on the right hand side – the heart side – is either heart zone or heart influenced, and everything on the left hand side – the head side – is either head zone or head influenced. And the board has a 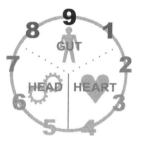 continuous vertical scale – from "direct engagement" at the top of the board, to "deep in the inner life" at the foot of the board.

The one great contrast on the board remains the contrast between the head side, for logic and reason, and the heart side, for emotions and dreams – with various degrees of the third "gut" influence filtering down from the top of the board.

We complete the pattern now as we move to the head zone.

Head types – introduction

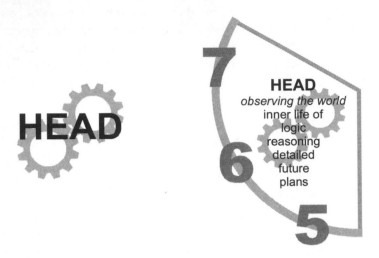

We have worked our way down the right hand side of the strategy board, from the gut zone at the top of the board, through the heart zone, to the very foot of the board on the heart side at FOUR. We now cross from the heart side to the head side, to make the journey back up the board, from the foot of the board on the head side at FIVE, back up the left hand side toward the gut zone where we began.

It is a strange symmetry between the head side and the heart side – as though the pattern is repeated but in contrasting colors and shades. FIVE, like FOUR, shows the effects of being far from the gut zone – particularly conscious of the inner life of head and heart, and a long way from the gut zone's direct, immediate, practical engagement with the world. SEVEN, like TWO, has a strong gut influence. And the pattern of heart types TWO and THREE and FOUR relating respectively to individuals, to groups and to the world is repeated in their respective symmetrical counterparts – SEVEN and SIX and FIVE. More generally, the head types share with the heart types the sense that there is a self within, then a boundary, then the world beyond, to which the self can relate – quite distinct from the gut approach, which is unselfconscious in its direct engagement with the world.

But here the contrasts begin. The head types like to lean out over that boundary: they find it natural to reach out to others, and need to learn how to protect and nurture the self. The head types prefer to observe the world from their own side of the boundary: they find it natural to protect and nurture the self, and choose from their place of safety whether and when to reach out to others.

The heart is often reliving past emotions and visions and dreams – in a timeframe that highlights the present and the past. The head is more often making detailed future plans – in a timeframe that highlights the present and the future.

The gut zone is about feelings – instinctive and immediate – and the heart zone is about feelings – emotional and contemplative. But the head zone is a place to think: a place for assessing and considering the world with objectivity, logic, and analysis; the home of observation, calculation, rationality, and language.

Stepping into that room full of strangers, the gut types immediately feel that they are a part of what is going on, and the heart types want to reach out and connect. In such a complex situation, the head types would rather be controlling the robot of the human form from the security of a watchtower where there is time and space to think and to plan, picking up the signals and sending back the commands.

That objective, logical, and rational place is the inner life of the head – and that is where we go now, into the head zone.

FIVE

HEAD + heart (FIVE)
"think it through first"

At FIVE we are once again down at the foot of the diagram – a long way from the gut zone and its direct engagement with the outside world. As a head-heart combination, FIVE is very conscious of the inner life of head and heart, and that inner life – rather than the outside world – is FIVE's natural home. The story of FIVE meeting the world is the story of FIVE's inner life seeking to engage with the outside world from which it feels distant and separate. So far, so similar to FOUR – but with FIVE, on the left hand side of the board, it is the head which takes the lead in the inner life of head and heart.

As a head type, FIVE likes to collect all the relevant data, and then apply logic and reason in planning how best to engage with the world. Of all the head types, FIVE is most conscious of this process, being the most conscious of the inner life, the most distant from the gut zone. FIVE is consciously observing the world from a distance, and analyzing, and seeking to understand, before deciding whether and how to engage. The added heart influence in FIVE has its own very specific effect: it adds a genuine concern about the many consequences of any decision to act. Head type FIVE resolves to approach the world with this main strategy: "think it through first". FIVE becomes a thinker and an observer, standing back, taking it all in, thinking it through, giving little away – self-consciously holding back from any over-hasty engagement with the world.

The challenge for FIVEs is to use what they have learned. Wanting to work it all out before acting, before engaging, is fine –

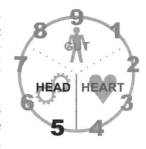

but even FIVE will never know everything, and the time will come when it is right nevertheless to act, to engage, or at the very least speak out. That is the challenge, and the risk, which FIVE must dare to take.

Failing to rise to the challenge, FIVE can end up completely disconnected from the world. FIVE corrupted can be aloof, withdrawn, and superior. At the extreme, all ability to act or engage with the world is gone: the door to the room in the ivory tower is locked and sealed. The temptation of FIVE is actually greed – not as excessive consumption but as hoarding and stinginess, "taking it all in and giving nothing away", born out of fear of the complex and ambiguous world outside.

When FIVE does rise to the challenge, the gift FIVE brings to the world is wisdom. Wisdom is knowledge distilled from all that has been collected, processed into applicable principles, and made available to all. With FIVE's gift of wisdom comes FIVE's gift of discernment, as FIVE understands systems and connections from a uniquely objective standpoint, making redeemed FIVE a unique resource of applicable wise counsel in complex human situations. FIVE has a unique objectivity, a wider perspective. Silent and therefore forgotten in the heated or meandering discussion, objective FIVE may quietly speak up at the end with the perfect solution that nobody else could see on account of their personal investment or involvement.

The cartoon animal for FIVE is the wise owl – looking down from some corner high above, all seeing, but unseen – or the fox, which knows the territory well, but disappears as soon as it is spotted – or the magpie, collecting interesting pieces and storing them away to ponder alone and at leisure.

FIVEs who use what they collect can be inventors, discoverers, and philosophers. They can be provocative, unorthodox, surprising, and profound. They are often unexpectedly humorous: observational humor is characteristically FIVE.

The national stereotype for FIVE is the British stiff upper lip – the middle-ranking officer or the Victorian father figure. This unfashionable past ideal can be a benevolent, dependable, stabilizing presence – keeping a place of calm and security and retreat, a place of safety and simple virtue in a hostile or complex world. The challenge to this icon is not to remain a mere silent presence when the challenge comes to engage: at that moment, redeemed FIVE will not withdraw and disappear, but calmly produce exactly the resources required, from all that has been stored away.

In the Bible, the Wisdom writers are often FIVE. Psalm 73 is a classic work of FIVE: it observes and describes with complete objectivity; then it ponders what it all might mean, seeking understanding; and then it rises to the occasion with a conclusion and a declaration.

For FIVEs, the path from corruption to redemption – from pointless withdrawal to valued source of wisdom – involves learning to engage with ordinary non-FIVE people and the wider world – even though it may still be ambiguous and uncertain, not yet fully observed and understood. This means stilling, or rising above, the endlessly churning mind, learning to see the wisdom in the ordinary, and even learning the art of small talk – demeaning and unworthy though it may at first appear. The wise owl discovers that even the simplest creature in the forest has its own form of wisdom: the deep insight is a bonus, not the essence; real wisdom may be more readily gained through engagement with the world than through ever more distant isolation. To support all of this, FIVEs, who are furthest of all from the gut zone, do need to remember three incarnational basics: to take some exercise, get some fresh air, and eat the right food.

FIVE (HEAD + heart)
Strategy: think it through first
Watching and taking it all in; thinking it through. Corrupt FIVEs can be aloof, withdrawn, isolated. Redeemed FIVEs can be wise and discerning, objective, understanding systems and connections, able to give generously from rich resources – to use what has been learned.
Temptation: greed – as in hoarding and stinginess
Gifts: wisdom, discernment
Animals: owl, fox, magpie
National stereotype: British stiff upper lip
In the Bible: Psalm 73
Paths to redemption: Engage with "ordinary" people and the wider world. Learn to love, not reject. See the wisdom in the ordinary. Rise above the churning mind. Take some exercise, get some fresh air, eat the right food.

SIX

HEAD

HEAD (SIX)

"stick with what you know"

At SIX we are in the middle of the head zone – the place of logic and reason. SIX gathers information as it goes along – and then uses that accumulated knowledge as the foundation on which to build its further interactions with the world around. Meeting the daily complexity of the world, the strategy of head type SIX is "stick with what you know."

There is an empowering confidence in this strategy. It asserts that if something is known, there is no need to fear: you take what you know, and you stay with it, you commit to it. Loyalty and faithfulness belong to SIX. SIX stays the course once a choice has been made. SIX is a point of stability: constant and dependable, the least swayed by passing emotions or unexpected developments, the one still standing at the end of the storm. Classic, enduring, loyal friendships are SIX. Dependable companionship is SIX.

SIX's faithful commitment to the ordinary business of life means that SIXes get things done – and do so without ever wishing to draw attention to themselves. For the church fete, while the other types are dreaming about revising the concepts behind the event or re-branding it or changing the whole approach, the SIXes are organizing trestle tables and repairing the games and printing the posters and making the jam and ensuring that the event will actually happen, like every year, on the day and at the time appointed.

In mainstream society, quietly getting things done, SIX – in the English vernacular – is "the salt of the earth," "a brick" – or "a rock" – holding to what is known and staying the course.

SIX is a team player, naturally at home in a group. A group functions perfectly as a defined "known world" within which SIX can operate with confidence. SIX can be an exemplary team member – loyal, reliable, committed, cooperative, even self-sacrificial, ready to take on a share of responsibility, and expecting others to do the same.

To make their strategy workable – to "stick with what they know" – SIXes do need clear boundaries. They need to know what counts as the safe area and what counts as the danger zone; what counts as known, and therefore safe, and what counts as unknown, and therefore unsafe; who is in the group, and therefore a known quantity, and who is not in the group, and therefore an unknown quantity; who is friend, and who is foe; who is with us, and who is not; what is compulsory, and what is not; what is permitted, and what is not. Within the known boundaries, SIXes can operate with absolute confidence and bring their unique gifts of loyalty, faithfulness, and commitment – but they do not like to have to go beyond those boundaries, they do not like to have to take the lead, and they do need to know where those boundaries lie.

It has sometimes been asserted that "God has a blueprint for your life" – whereby God has determined in advance who you should marry, where you should live, what you should do for work and for leisure, the color of your kitchen, and the menu for dinner tonight. In this view of the world, the definition of sin is any deviation from the daily blueprint. Everything is either forbidden or compulsory: there is nothing optional in between.

This is a very fearful, "corrupted SIX" view of the world – with the boundaries drawn very tightly. A healthier SIX knows that beyond the compulsory, and before the forbidden, lies a realm where it is "known" to be both safe and permitted to explore, to run free – where the richness of life can be lived to the full with confidence and freedom and creativity. Part of the challenging dynamic for SIX is defining and redefining where the relevant boundaries lie.

Daring to draw a boundary wider is a life-changing experience for SIX – for example: the definition of who is safely Christian could

be expanded from the membership list of one strict denomination to include "all those who can name Jesus as Lord"; the definition of worthy and valuable fellow human beings could be extended from the residents of one village or district or national group to include the entire human race of every continent and creed. These are daring redefinitions which liberate SIX – more than any other type – to go forward with confidence into new or unexplored areas and discover whole new aspects of life, using their gifts of loyalty and commitment ever more widely. The sense of "home" – the old boundary – can remain as the final place of safety, but a whole new world has opened up within the new and wider boundary.

With their clarity of thought and their nose for danger, SIXes can be far-sighted and discerning as they work with others on future plans. SIXes often need to trust more and to fear less – but there are times when their reciprocal gift to others is to point out well in advance where danger may lie.

The national stereotype for SIX is rural white America – "the American red neck" – fiercely loyal to the farm, the family, the village, possibly the county – and deeply suspicious of all else.

The cartoon animal for SIX could be anything which operates with loyalty and efficiency in a group – whether a pack or a shoal or a flock. Think of the starlings that arrive on the lawn – first a half dozen, then twenty, then forty, then a hundred and more – and take flight together in an instant at the first unfamiliar sound. Or think of the geese that can fly together for thousands of miles – always in the same familiar "V" formation – taking it in turns to take the lead. Working together in this way almost doubles their potential range. Those taking a turn further back in the formation honk to encourage those taking a turn up front. And if one becomes weak or takes an injury, a small group will break off to stay with the weaker bird and continue later – in their own, smaller, "V" formation. On the ground geese are fiercely protective of their own. Confidence, loyalty, and faithfulness.

In the Bible, Peter shows us SIX – a complex mixture of loyalty and fear. He is one of the core group of loyal disciples, alongside Jesus at all the key moments in three years of itinerant ministry – and yet fear repeatedly prevents him from achieving his best: fear of sinking, fear of what lies ahead in Jerusalem, fear of what is happening as Maundy Thursday night becomes Good Friday morning – although even then, his loyalty keeps him well within sight of the courthouse. Jesus gives Peter a wonderful SIX name – the Rock – for the best of the gifts of SIX – which flourish in Peter after Pentecost. Those gifts of SIX are confidence and loyalty and faithfulness – within the realm of what is known.

And the temptations of SIX are cowardice – the fear of the unknown – and sometimes the active condemnation of anything unfamiliar. Sometimes life challenges us to move beyond what we already know.

The path from corruption to redemption for SIX involves questioning and dismantling some of those boundaries: learning not to have to ask permission; learning to trust God and self a little instead of just the dry old rules; learning to trust more, and to fear less. On the path from corruption to redemption, SIXes learn to talk to God like a perfect loyal friend, and learn to have fun, laugh a little, and enjoy the potential richness of life.

SIX (HEAD) – **Strategy:** stick with what you know
Confident and committed within the bounds of their known world – and clear about what is known and what is not. Corrupt SIXes can be simultaneously self-righteous and insecure, fearful of the unknown. Redeemed SIXes are loyal, responsible, dependable team players – generous, far-sighted, discerning, encouraging.

Temptation: cowardice, fear
Gifts: faithfulness, confidence, commitment, loyalty
Animal: flight of geese
National stereotype: American red neck
In the Bible: Peter
Paths to redemption: Learn not to have to ask permission. Learn to trust God and self a little. Talk to God like a friend. Dismantle some boundaries: expand your horizons.

SEVEN

HEAD + gut (SEVEN)

"stay positive come what may"

SEVEN is a head type, logical and rational – but with added gut influence, which invites it to engage with the world. So it is that head type SEVEN has a calculated determination to be practical and direct. And then – it is only logical – to continue being practical and direct, whatever may happen.

SEVEN has lessons to teach us all about how to keep going through good times and bad. The key is to stay positive: the strategy of SEVEN is "stay positive, come what may" – a head strategy in the service of direct engagement with the world.

Our unpredictable world brings mixed blessings to everyone – but there is always something for which to give thanks, no matter how small it may be. SEVENs choose to find it. SEVENs are full of gratitude for the past and for the present, and full of optimism for the future. This is what gives SEVENs so much positive energy – which they bring to their own situations, and share with others as well. The gift of SEVEN is a joy that SEVENs can share. It can be a delight simply to be with them. They lift your spirits and send you on your way rejoicing at the blessings all around you.

The challenge for upbeat, optimistic SEVENs is to be honest with themselves and with others about the negative things in the world: to deal somehow with the realities of sadness and pain. SEVEN corrupt is often running away from the pain or denying its existence – but it may catch them up or trip them up in the end. In contrast, SEVEN redeemed has stopped running, turned to face the harder realities, stared them in the eye, and declared: "I will not be defeated by you."

Corrupt SEVEN can be like the British circus clown – amusing for half an hour at a children's party, but you would not want any more. Redeemed SEVEN is like the silent French pantomime clown Pierrot, with that tear painted on the whitened cheek: genuinely good humored and entertaining at the children's party – and  then movingly silent, and a strong and comforting presence, when the situation demands.

The national stereotype for SEVEN is the Irish pub or wake. There is great pain in the history of the nation, and even in the present. There will be absolute silence as Grandma in the corner sings the most beautiful lament – and the perfect pause to "hold the moment" – and then it's time to pour some more Guinness, strike up the music, and dance another jig, despite everything. And being right next to the gut zone, SEVEN has easy access to many of the simple immediate pleasures of life: color, fresh air, good food, good company.

Their optimism for the future means that SEVENs will try their hand at anything, so they tend to acquire all manner of skills: SEVENs have been called "generalists" – versatile people with many talents. Inevitably some SEVENs are slightly reckless in their optimism, very good at starting things off, and rather less good at seeing them through. SEVENs can end up surrounded by projects begun and never completed.

One cartoon for SEVEN is the monkey: constantly moving from one thing to another, always active, bringing a rather clumsy lightness into any situation. Another is the butterfly, also constantly on the move, but gentler, with a much lighter touch, bringing color, a different kind of "lightness," and a simple delight.

While the gift of SEVEN is joy, the temptations of SEVEN are gluttony and excess. Without redeemed SEVEN's confidence to face the pain, SEVEN lives in fear of what life may bring next. If the present moment is cheerful, it will be extended at all costs –

another dessert, another drink, another joke, another song: everything must be a party, more is always better, and too much is never enough.

Characteristic of SEVEN – for good or for ill – is careful, detailed planning to ensure only happy moments in the day ahead. And SEVENs sometimes create a protective barrier by filling their environment with their own output – an excess of their own output – so that nothing painful can get in: SEVEN may be talking but not listening, acting but not watching.

In the Bible the rich young ruler is SEVEN. He already has not only all the wealth and prestige of the world but also plenty of religion – "all these I have kept from my youth" – and yet, all SEVEN, he comes to Jesus asking for more: "what must I do to inherit eternal life?" Jesus spots a SEVEN, and gives the advice that SEVEN needs: set yourself free from your props, your excess, the things which you are using to avoid the real challenges of life. "Sell your possessions, and give to the poor" (Matthew 19:16-21).

SEVENs on the path from corruption to redemption slow down to address the whole of life – not just the radiant side. They come to see the beauty and the joy in simple things – not just in excess. They no longer flee from the challenges of life, but meet them with a confident determination. They learn that God accepts the tears as well as the joy. A beautiful redeemed and redeeming role for SEVENs is to work with the suffering, perhaps with the sick and the dying: in this, they directly face and challenge all the pain of the world – and take their gift of joy to those who need it the most.

versatile
optimistic
stay positive JOY *superficiality*
come what may Solomon
living life to the full *gluttony*
Irish pub or wake excess
butterfly

SEVEN (HEAD + gut)
Strategy: stay positive come what may
Happy and versatile optimists, cheerful and positive. Corrupt SEVENs may be avoiding hard issues with a superficial cheerfulness. Redeemed SEVENs directly confront life's challenges – and live life to the full in the very face of them.
Temptation: gluttony (excess consumption)
Gift: joy
Animals: monkey, butterfly
National stereotype: Irish pub or wake
In the Bible: rich young ruler, Solomon (examined in Part 3)
Paths to redemption: Slow down to address the whole of life. See the beauty and the joy in simple things. Face the hard issues. Recognize that God accepts the whole – not just the radiant side.

Head types – review

HEAD
observing the world
inner life of
logic
reasoning
detailed
future
plans

Positive SEVEN's long list of friends is a list of distinct one-to-one relationships, very much like TWO's – but SEVEN engages in each with the logic of the head long before any engagement with the passion of the heart.

The group experience for team leader THREE is about passions, emotions, and dreams – but for team member SIX it is about logic, reason, and choice.

And intriguing symmetrical neighbors FOUR and FIVE, deep in the inner life, have much in common: both can have great insight and great objectivity; both plan carefully, even when pretending spontaneity; both can be tempted to withdraw from the world – but for FIVE, all of this experience is primarily in the head, while for FOUR it is primarily in the heart. FIVE and FOUR can both experience inner turmoil: for FOUR it is in the churning emotions, for FIVE it is in the churning mind. And while FOUR is seeking a profound and "emotionally complete" understanding of the past, FIVE is consciously planning and choosing a future.

Where the heart zone was a place for emotions and dreams – reaching out at TWO and THREE and FOUR – the head zone is a place to think and decide – observing and deciding at SEVEN and SIX and FIVE.

To bring their best gifts, the head types need to overcome the fear that lives in their heads, and trust more – in God and in their own giftedness. Then, with heart and gut engaged so far as they are able, they may dare to step out in faith: FIVEs step out into action, SIXes step out beyond the inherited boundaries, and SEVENs step out toward the whole of life, not just the glittering part of it. And still their best gifts are right there in their own home sectors: wisdom, and faithfulness, and joy.

The Head Types

The Strategy Board – all nine sectors

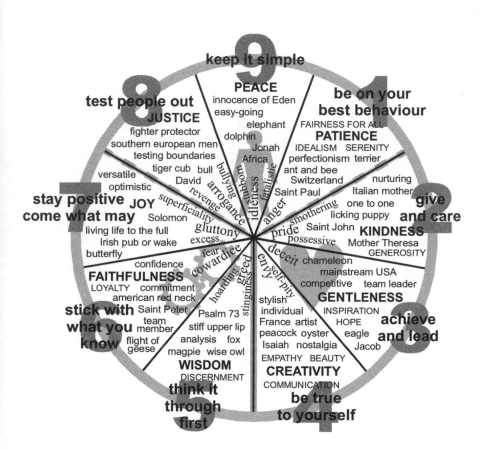

Discerning home base – Part 1

Each of the nine strategies taken separately reads like a piece of good advice. All nine may be good advice in different situations. One of the nine may even be a favorite piece of "advice to yourself" – which you repeat to yourself like a proverb and make a conscious effort to follow. Following this favorite piece of "advice to yourself" may take some effort – but it extends the range of what you can do.

If it takes some effort, and it extends the range of what you can do, it is almost certainly not your home base strategy. Your home base strategy is the advice you never needed to be given, the approach that comes most naturally, the strategy you use automatically without pausing to consider or decide. Your favorite piece of advice to yourself – requiring some effort and extending the range of what you can do – is far more likely to be one of the pieces of advice diametrically opposite your home base on the board. The strategy that comes naturally, and the advice that you drill yourself to follow, are opposites in concept – and opposites on the board. Only if you had spent years away from home base, for whatever reason, would you need to give yourself the "advice" of home base – and it would feel wonderfully effortless and natural – like a homecoming – whenever you took it.

Your attitude to your home base strategy is more likely to be one of rebellion than choice. You identify some version of your underlying strategy as the source of your worst temptations, and rebel against it, determining to use a different approach. But that new approach will never come naturally: it will always be an effort in itself – and in reality it has its own pitfalls, just like the natural approach you are trying to escape. Despite its temptations, it is your natural home base sector that reveals your true gifting and vocation – and while you may travel widely, it is the only place that will ever "feel like home".

Gifts and temptations

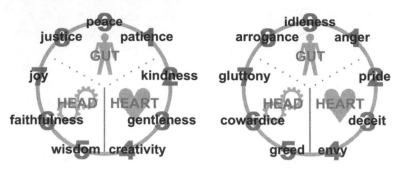

People are often completely unaware of their own most natural gifts. Your "home base" gifts may be such a natural part of every ordinary day that you have never thought to remark on them or name them or consider them in any way special or unusual. Once you find your place on the strategy board, you may be able to name your gifts, and give thanks for them, and use them day by day in a whole new creative way: each person is invited to "claim" the gift that is already theirs.

You will also have been living with your home base temptation day by day and year by year. It is the one temptation you have fought more than any other. You have years of accumulated expertise in suppressing it, hiding it, justifying and denying it. You may have become convinced that it is the one temptation from the list that you do not face, you have spent so much time dealing with it. And yet, included in the description of the sector which otherwise seems to be yours, it could be staring at you again, unwelcome, repeatedly confronted, but somehow still there. Admitting the home base temptation can be the hardest thing – but it is the best possible launch onto the journey to redemption. The temptation is only the corruption of the strategy. The strategy itself is neutral, and can be turned to good. Name the temptation, and you are liberated to use your strategy positively to reach for your gifts. Acknowledging the temptation brings the freedom to move on from fallenness into giftedness.

Developing all three resources

As well as dealing with the temptation and "claiming" the gift, the path to redemption will involve making use of all of our God-given resources: head and heart and gut.

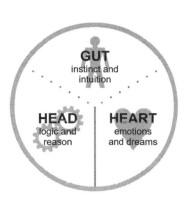

It is the different balance of influences from head and heart and gut in each of us that makes us the diverse people that we are – with all of our diverse gifts – but we all have at least something of all three resources, and there is value in making use of them all.

The gut types EIGHT and NINE and ONE can be so focused on engaging with the world in a direct and practical way that they miss the potential value of careful and logical planning – from the head – and relationship building – from the heart. This way lie the temptations to arrogance and idleness and anger. Developing the skills of head and heart improves relationships with others – and actually helps bring out the gifts of the gut zone, which are justice and reconciliation and idealism.

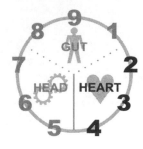

The heart types TWO and THREE and FOUR can be so focused on relationship building, and on their own emotions and dreams, that they miss the importance, for themselves and for those around them, of careful and logical planning – the business of the head zone – and practical action in the world – the business of the gut zone. This way lie the temptations to pride and deceit and envy. Adding in some head-zone logical planning and some gut-zone direct engagement with the world will ultimately help to bring out the full potential of the heart-zone gifts of kindness and gentleness and creativity.

The head types FIVE and SIX and SEVEN can be so focused on logic and reason and planning for the future that they miss the importance of gut-zone practicality and heart-zone relationship building in the present. The result can be an "illogical" level of hoarding, cowardice, and gluttony – and head types can also lose touch with their own "feelings" in both the heart zone and the gut zone. A full head-zone analysis of any situation is complemented – or perhaps we should just say completed – by attention to intuition and practicalities in the gut zone, and to emotional and relational issues in the heart zone. Developing the heart and gut resources will ultimately help to bring out the positive head-zone gifts of wisdom and faithfulness and joy.

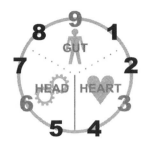

For THREE and SIX and NINE, each in the center of a zone, there are clearly two more resources to develop in order to make use of all three resources. The other sectors – ONE and TWO, and FOUR and FIVE, and SEVEN and EIGHT – already have both a home zone and a secondary influence. It is the third remaining resource that most needs development.

FOUR and FIVE are the head-heart combinations, furthest from the gut zone. They both live richly in the inner life, and the challenge is to engage more directly with the outside world. This is the gift of the gut zone – that part of every person that can indeed be unselfconscious and immediate and practical and direct. The temptations of FOUR and FIVE – envy, and a hoarding of resources – both come from a feeling of being very separate from the world. Engaging with the world a little more – with the instinct and intuition and practical immediacy of the gut zone – can help to bring out the creativity and communication and discernment and wisdom which are the true gifts of FOUR and FIVE.

ONE and TWO are the heart-gut combinations, furthest from the head zone. The combination of heart and gut has both ONE and TWO engaging fairly directly with the world but with a strong emotional influence. This can make ONEs and TWOs alike quite impulsive: TWOs rush in to help whoever appears to be in need, often without a further thought, and perfectionist ONEs can be very judgmental – also without pausing for thought. Developing the objectivity and rational planning of the head can help to bring out the gift of patience in ONE's idealism, and more practical effectiveness and sensitivity in TWO's acts of kindness and generosity.

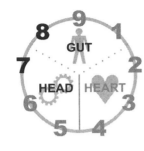

Finally SEVEN and EIGHT are the head-gut combinations, furthest from the heart zone. The combination of head and gut has both SEVEN and EIGHT engaging fairly directly with the world but with a strong influence from the head: EIGHT can analyze what is going on, and often knows exactly what to do next; SEVEN finds the positive in any situation, and locks on to it. These are empowering strategies, but if SEVEN and EIGHT are too "heartless," they can become "headstrong": EIGHT can be quite aggressive and confrontational; and if SEVEN is glossing over the difficult and the painful, the upbeat energy of SEVEN can be hurtful for those who do confront those issues or feel that pain. It is connecting with the heart that can most surely help EIGHT to avoid the temptation of arrogance, and become instead the protector of the weak and the fighter for justice – the gift and the talent and the vocation of EIGHT. And it is connecting with the heart that can most surely help SEVEN to avoid the inward-looking temptation of excess and discover instead the outward-looking gift of a joy to share with others – specifically a joy that overcomes, rather than denies, the pain. For SEVEN and EIGHT alike, home base is still a powerful and valuable head-gut combination – testing things out and choosing the positive – but developing the heart helps bring out the full richness of the special gifts of these two sectors – justice and joy.

Taking the advice of the opposites

The home base strategy is "what comes naturally." It draws on your most dominant resources.

The two strategies directly opposite home base are likely to be strategies that do not come naturally at all, as they draw on your least dominant resources.

And with all nine strategies being pieces of good advice in different situations, the strategies directly opposite home base – the two strategies that do not come naturally at all – may well be the pieces of advice most worthy of special effort and attention.

Strategy:
keep it simple

Advice:
Think it through first.
Be true to yourself.

Gut type NINE can often be trapped by inertia, or swept along by the crowd "for the sake of an easy life." It is good advice for gut type NINE to stop and think things through first, and try to "be true to yourself." These are the two strategies that draw on both head and heart – NINE's least dominant resources – at FOUR and FIVE on the board, directly opposite NINE.

Strategy:
achieve and lead

Advice:
Test people out.
Stay positive come
what may.

Heart type THREE often invests a huge amount in a network of relationships – and not every "investment" will prove wise or beneficial. It can often be good advice for THREE to try to "test people out" a little before investing too much – and, should a relationship turn sour, not to sink into despair but to keep going and "stay positive, come what may." These are the strategies that draw on both head and gut, at SEVEN and EIGHT on the board: not always easy for heart type THREE, but good advice – complementing the dominant heart influence.

Strategy:
stick with what you
know

Advice:
Be on your best
behavior.
Give and care.

Head type SIX functions best with the familiar. It is a challenge for SIX to venture out into the unknown, and there is a danger that SIX can become reactionary or insular. The advice most needed by SIX is the advice of heart and gut acting together at ONE and TWO: when venturing out into the unknown, a direct engagement characterized by courtesy and politeness and generosity and caring will often serve you well – and these are the heart and gut strategies of ONE and TWO.

The logic is the same for the remaining six sectors, which each have a primary and a secondary influence: the two opposites for each type provide valuable advice.

Strategy:
be on your best
behavior

Advice:
Think it through first.
Stick with what you
know.

ONE, for example, is the gut type with a secondary heart influence. The head is the resource held in reserve. It is often good advice for gut-plus-heart ONE consciously to choose the head strategy, SIX, or the head-plus-heart strategy, FIVE, as pieces of good advice. In both cases, ONE is developing ONE's less dominant resources. In practical terms: ONE often acts impulsively or judgmentally, according to some rule of conscience or etiquette, without really thinking through the consequences. It can therefore be good advice for ONE to adopt the natural caution of FIVE and SIX – "think it through first," and "stick with what you know."

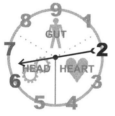

Strategy:
give and care

Advice:
Stick with what you
know. Stay positive
come what may.

The spontaneous generosity of heart-plus-gut TWOs can often leave them over-committed, so "stick with what you know" – the head advice at SIX – is good advice for TWO. And TWOs can often be hurt, having so much generously invested in their relationships with others: "stay positive come what may" – head-plus-gut advice at SEVEN, can also be good advice for TWO.

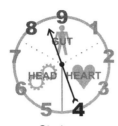

Strategy:
be true to yourself

Advice:
Test people out.
Keep it simple.

Strategy:
think it through first

Advice:
Keep it simple. Be on
your best behavior.

FOUR's natural strategy – "be true to yourself" – can leave heart type FOUR vulnerable when choosing to be open with others. Testing people out a little first – the advice of EIGHT – can protect against this, and can help sensitive FOUR to be a little more thick-skinned when that is necessary for self-protection. FOURs can also suffer from an inhibiting inner turmoil, and the strategy of NINE is then good advice: edit out all the unnecessary complications; keep it simple.

FIVE can also suffer from an inner turmoil – more of the mind than the emotions – and again, the advice of NINE is good advice: sometimes it is best to edit out the complications and keep it simple in order to engage effectively with the world. And another piece of good advice for head type FIVE – often tied up in the distant inner world of observation and calculation – is the gut-plus-heart advice of ONE: to keep with the etiquette of the world outside, trusting at least some of its established wisdom, and taking care as a minimum to be courteous and polite.

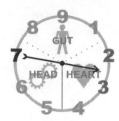

Strategy:
stay positive come
what may

Advice:
Achieve and lead.
Give and care.

SEVEN's talent for finding the positive in every situation often sees SEVEN responding to situations rather than creating them. There are times – including for SEVEN – when it is good and right to take a lead and deliberately influence or change a situation: this is what comes naturally to THREE, and the advice "achieve and lead" can be good advice for SEVEN. Bringing joy into a situation where there is no joy may mean taking a lead. And determining to achieve some clear goals – like THREE – may encourage SEVEN to finish off at least some of those many tasks which have been so enthusiastically begun. And when the temptation of SEVEN is gluttony and excess, the remedy to that can be to look away from the self and toward others – taking the advice at TWO, to give and to care.

Strategy:
test people out

Advice:
Achieve and lead.
Be true to yourself.

EIGHT can get caught up in kicking every boundary and every rule in a destructive way – fighting against things rather than achieving things or taking a positive lead. The advice at THREE may be good advice: to achieve something, to try to give a positive and constructive lead; to woo people sometimes, like THREE, as well as confronting them as EIGHT. And part of the challenge for EIGHT, out there in the gut zone, is to discover the inner life, especially of the heart: to discover the emotional heart of the self behind the battling exterior, and to be true to that self – the advice at FOUR.

The path to redemption – Part 1

In these sections we have plotted for all nine sectors a "generic" path to redemption:

- deal with the temptation
- claim the gift
- make use of all three resources (head and heart and gut)
- take the advice of the opposites

The journey will be very different for each of the nine types, but the logic is consistent: it is all about the action and the interaction of these three resources – head and heart and gut.

For some people, there is one more key step – and it needs to go at the top of the list, not on the end of it. People who have spent years away from home base – for whatever reason – need to find their way back home.

There are many reasons why a person may try to function as if they belonged to a sector other than their own. There may be social pressure. The situation may demand a particular approach. And yet it is in each person's home base sector that their best gifts and their true vocation will be found. For some, the first and best step on the path to redemption will be "finding their way back home" – discovering, and then learning to value and affirm, the gifts which are truly theirs. There is more on this stage of the journey in Part 2.

Celebrating all of who we are

For most of the two thousand years of Church history, and for years before that in Rome and in Greece and beyond, written and taught philosophy and theology have been largely the preserve of the head types. As a consequence, much that is historically written and taught praises the virtues of the objective mind and warns against the wickedness and vanity of the "passions" of the body and the heart.

Perhaps it is in reaction to this that many spiritual writers and teachers in the present age are celebrating the gifts of our incarnation – our embodiment, our gut – and the gifts of the heart – love and emotion.

Many books on prayer now speak of the need to find a relaxed posture, to breathe slowly and deeply, to release every physical tension, perhaps to use some simple symbol to help "focus" and "center down": this is one great celebration of our embodiment, our incarnation – the body and the gut zone.

Discipleship and pilgrimage are often now described in terms of love and love and love – for God, for neighbor, for one another, even for the self – a great celebration of the heart zone – rather than in heady lists of specific virtues or duties.

Churches are being built or reordered to look less like lecture theatres and more like meeting places for human communities. More and more churches are making the Eucharist, rather than "a service of the word," the main service of the day. Some Christians are even learning how to dance.

To be complete, the earthly, human Church of God needs all the gifts that God has given in making us the human children of God – all the gifts of all three of the distinct but interacting zones that define the whole human person: the head, the heart, and the body or gut. This is how God has made us: the human form in God's own image – so perfect that God could dwell in it in Christ – in body, head, and heart.

Neurology

And finally in Part 1 – the strategy board and the human brain.

The strategy board is a map of humankind. It is also a map of the individual. Both emerge from the strategy board's simple mapping of three human experiences – those we call "head" and "heart" and "gut."

All three of these human experiences can be traced in the human brain. And the three are arranged in the brain in a logical and practical and orderly fashion – just as they are on the strategy board. The strategy board – is a map of the human brain.

The brain is essentially a concentration of nerve tissue at the top end – the front end – of the spinal cord. The parts closest to the spinal cord specialize in the essentials of life support: breathing, heartbeat, hunger, thirst, pleasure, and pain. Next come those parts responsible for the control of the body in terms of sensation, movement, and learned physical skills. All of these functions tend to straddle the boundary between conscious and unconscious thought. We rarely think in detail about the physical movements involved in breathing, or in picking up a cup, or even in changing gear while driving. We do not need to calculate consciously that a particular pattern of colors and shapes represents a familiar table or door – or that a particular series of sounds means that the door is about to open. We are talking about functions that belong in the realm of instinct and intuition and direct action. This is the brain of the gut zone.

As we move further away from the spinal cord into the higher brain or forebrain, further into the uniquely large cerebrum of the human brain, we enter those parts of the human brain concerned with conscious thought and emotion and memory and planning. These processes of the brain are less concerned with direct physical sensation and movement, and more concerned with the breadth of complex experiences and conscious choices, which make the human race unique. Furthest of all from the spinal cord are the frontal lobes, concerned entirely with abstract, analytical, and conceptual thought, and not at all with the sensations and control of the body.

The cerebrum is famously divided into two by a deep central fissure. The resultant left brain and right brain are well connected to each other, but they remain distinct: each side is better connected to the lower or rear parts of the brain than to the other side.

Each side of the brain manages sensation and action in one side of the body – but even so, the brain is not entirely symmetrical across this central divide. The left brain and the right brain have different higher specializations. The left brain looks after language and logic: the inner life of the "head." The right brain looks after complex emotions and non-verbal concepts and images and dreams: the inner life of the "heart."

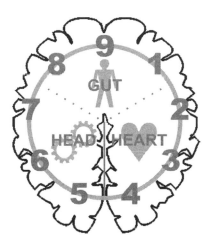

Place the strategy board diagram on the wall, and place the crown of your head against the diagram, and you have a remarkably accurate map of the human brain.

FOURs and FIVEs, our artists and philosophers, self-consciously separate from the outside world – observing it from afar, distilling wisdom, and abstracting concepts – are the people whose dominant center of thought is all the way out in the frontal lobes.

More generally, our heart types have their dominant center of thought in the right brain – all emotions and concepts and images – and our head types have their dominant center of thought in the left brain, all language and logic. THREE, in the middle of the right brain, is the expert at picking up the nuances of a complex group situation and acting on them. SIX, in the middle of the left brain, is very precisely where language and logic reside. TWO is in the right brain, full of emotion, but closer to the rear brain, taking direct engaging action. SEVEN is in the left brain, planning and deciding, also closer to the rear brain, concerned with pleasure and pain.

We must not undervalue or underestimate the intelligence of the lower or rear brain. Analysis and calculation go on there in a place inaccessible to the consciousness – but with no less accuracy or insight for that. Only the result is sent out to the conscious brain – producing the phenomenon that leads us to say "I just know it in my gut" or "in my bones" or "in my blood." These are the instincts and

intuitions of the directly engaging gut types – EIGHT and NINE and ONE. Many successful business people know full well that they only write up detailed "left brain" business plans in order to justify to their superiors and bankers "what they just know in their bones": for some people, their best thinking goes on right back there where the consciousness cannot reach. NINE's instincts are right there at the center. ONE's instincts add in that right brain influence of sensitivity to the approval or disapproval of others. EIGHT's instincts add in that left brain influence – learning about the world by testing things out.

And so it seems that in using these three resources, these three "centers of intelligence" – "head" and "heart" and "gut" – we are using three distinct resources of the human brain.

For whatever reason, we each tend to rely on one of the three more than the others. How we do use the others – equally or unequally – produces a pattern of nine ways of working: nine patterns of influence from these three distinct zones. The main contrast is left brain versus right brain – across that central divide – and the other contrast is how far backward or forward we are working: close to the actual sensations and actions of the body in the world, or far away from sensation and action, in abstract thought. These are our resources, and our different patterns of using them make us the diverse people that we are.

There may be elements of both "nature" and "nurture" in determining who we become: genetic factors may influence which parts of the brain become most dominant, and there may be "nurture" factors as well. At the strictly physical level, there may be some asymmetry of brain development determined by non-genetic physical factors – how we lie in the uterus, or a bump on the head. And at the microscopic neurological level, it is known that storing information, or learning a skill, actually causes physical changes in the brain. Perhaps our consistent use of one strategy early in life actually locks us into that strategy through physical changes in the brain. But no harm is done: however it may come about, we become experts, practiced in our own strategy – and we have unique gifts to bring to the world. Our strategy becomes a fundamental part of who we are, and our spiritual journey is not to change who we are, but to find, in our walk with God, our unique God-given redemption and vocation and gifts.

Part 2:

Wings and Moves
and other functions

Wings and moves – introduction

Everyone has a usual strategy – one of the nine – which is their most common approach to any new situation.

But the most common approach is not the only approach. In addition to their usual strategy, everyone has a range of alternative strategies for approaching different situations.

Within the infinite variety of humankind, each individual will use their alternative strategies to different degrees – but clear patterns do emerge.

There are alternative strategies within reach of each sector, which do not involve moving away from that sector at all. These alternative strategies are called the "wings." They involve only minor adjustments in each sector's balance of influences from head and heart and gut.

The other alternative strategies involve more significant changes in the usual balance of influences: in effect, they represent moves to another part of the board altogether, at least for a while. These alternatives strategies are called the "moves" – and they tend to follow a distinctive pattern of well-trodden paths across the board.

The wings – the neighboring sectors

NINE is in the center of the gut zone. The gut is NINE's primary influence – and the source of NINE's usual strategy, "keep it simple." Head and heart are kept equally "in reserve."

When NINE is looking for an alternative strategy, the most natural thing is for the gut to remain the dominant influence while one of the other resources – usually kept in reserve – comes into play as a temporary secondary influence.

When the head comes into play as the secondary influence, it gives gut type NINE the combination of influences – "gut plus head" – that we usually refer to as EIGHT. And the result is the use of strategy EIGHT, "test people out." All the usual consequences of strategy EIGHT follow: the temptations, and the gifts, and the characteristic traits, of sector EIGHT.

And when the heart comes into play as the secondary influence, it gives gut type NINE the combination of influences – "gut plus heart" – that we usually refer to as ONE – and the result is the use of strategy ONE, "be on your best behavior." All the usual consequences of strategy ONE follow: the temptations, and the gifts, and the characteristic traits, of sector ONE.

These two neighboring sectors – EIGHT and ONE – are called the "wings" of NINE. NINE is still NINE, in sector NINE – but there is easy and natural access to the strategies and temptations and gifts and traits of the two wings.

The same logic applies in the center of the head zone, where SIX has the head-zone wings FIVE and SEVEN; and again in the center of the heart zone, where THREE has the heart-zone wings TWO and FOUR.

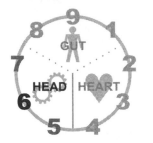 

In each case, there is just a minor change in the balance of influences from head and heart and gut: the primary influence – usually working alone – is complemented by one of the reserve resources.

A similar logic applies where a person's usual strategy derives not from a single influence but from a combination of two influences.

For ONE, the gut is the primary influence, but the heart is a clear secondary influence.

Looking for an alternative strategy, gut type ONE may drop the secondary heart influence and rely for a while on the gut influence alone: strategy NINE would then emerge, along with its usual consequences in terms of temptations and gifts and other characteristic traits.

Alternatively, ONE might allow the primary gut influence and the secondary heart influence to swap places for a while: strategy TWO would then emerge, along with all of its usual consequences in terms of temptations and gifts and other characteristic traits.

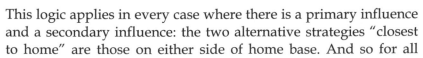

This logic applies in every case where there is a primary influence and a secondary influence: the two alternative strategies "closest to home" are those on either side of home base. And so for all nine types the immediately neighboring sectors – the "wings" – are the most easily accessible "alternative strategies," whenever the occasion arises to try an alternative approach.

One way of describing the "wings" effect is to say that the types "overlap" – but for all this overlapping, the nine types do remain distinct. ONE and TWO, for example, may have much in common, but they do not collapse into a single type. It is in the very nature of ONE to have aspects not only of TWO but also of NINE – and it is in the very nature of TWO to have aspects not only of ONE but also of THREE. ONE itself will have very little of THREE; and TWO will have very little of NINE.

This is how the wings might look for each of the nine types in turn.

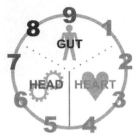

EIGHT has wings SEVEN and NINE

EIGHTs, who challenge the world around them, may do so with tireless energy – an aspect of SEVEN in EIGHT – confronting the world's unnecessary and unjust complexity – an aspect of NINE in EIGHT. But EIGHTs love to be bad: there is nothing here of the two types immediately beyond the wings, which are rule-bound SIX and conscience-driven ONE.

NINE has wings EIGHT and ONE

NINEs, engaging directly with the world, may choose to keep it simple by confronting whatever they meet – the EIGHT wing of NINE. Or they may keep it simple by being on their best behavior and keeping a low profile – the ONE wing of NINE. Whatever their approach, NINEs do meet the world directly as it is, without the complexity of the head work of SEVEN, or the emotional heart work of TWO – the next sectors along beyond the two wings.

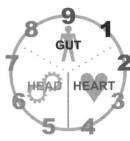

**ONE has wings
NINE and TWO**

Being on one's best behavior – for ONE – is a strategy applicable to virtually all situations: it keeps it simple, an aspect of NINE in ONE. The compassionate instinct of TWO is also likely to be a natural part of ONE's "best behavior" strategy – although for ONEs, the inner standards and conscience provide the main energy and drive, whereas for TWOs it is the perceived external needs that dominate. ONEs "on their best behavior" will not naturally make a priority of motivating or impressing the gathered crowd like THREEs – and they find it very difficult to do the EIGHT thing: to stop being polite and confront instead. ONE can naturally have the wings NINE and TWO, but not easily the next sectors along, which are EIGHT and THREE.

**TWO has wings
ONE and THREE**

Compassionate, giving, and caring TWOs will often choose being conventionally good as the best strategy – the ONE wing in TWO – particularly in anything other than a one-to-one situation, the context in which TWOs feel most at home. But TWOs can extend their compassion from individuals to a group, and they would love a group's recognition or respect – and this is the THREE wing in TWO. Comparing the sectors beyond the wings, TWOs are fairly directly engaged with their situation – unlike the more detached FOURs – and they log and manage and ponder every detail of their one-to-one relationships when they are alone – quite unlike "easy come, easy go" NINEs, who just engage on the day.

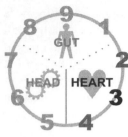

**THREE has wings
TWO and FOUR**

**FOUR has wings
THREE and FIVE**

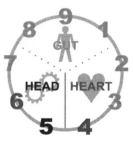

**FIVE has wings
FOUR and SIX**

THREEs' skills and expertise in group dynamics can also emerge as compassion and emotion one-to-one – the TWO wing in THREE – and can create the ability to communicate profoundly – the FOUR wing in THREE. THREE takes its cues from the group around – quite unlike the internal standards of ONE – and THREE responds to those cues directly: there is no FIVEish hesitation to think it all through first.

FOURs share with FIVEs their sense of detachment from the world, and with THREEs the ability to create something which is valued by many – but they cannot naturally manage a vast range of unconnected one-to-one relationships like TWOs, and as the world itself seems so distant for FOURs, its detailed boundaries and rules seem utterly irrelevant – there is nothing here of SIX.

FIVEs, thinking it all through before they act, are certainly natural neighbors of SIX, who stick with what they know – and they can share not only the detachment of FOURs, but also aspects of FOURs' creativity – usually in ideas but also in images and dreams. Looking immediately beyond the two wings, detached and withdrawn FIVE is far from being the natural group leader at THREE, or the constantly active SEVEN.

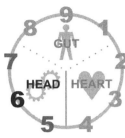

**SIX has wings
FIVE and SEVEN**

**SEVEN has wings
SIX and EIGHT**

SIXes will often feel blessed and contented within the boundaries of the world that they know – an aspect of SEVEN in SIX. And sticking with what they know, SIXes will often want to think things through in some detail – before acting or moving a boundary – an aspect of FIVE in SIX. Beyond the wings, neither the detached individualism of FOUR, nor the aggressive rule-breaking of EIGHT, fits the pattern of SIX at all.

Finally SEVENs, resolving to stay positive, are choosing to stay with what they know – an aspect of SIX in SEVEN – and they may take on aggressively – the EIGHT wing – every challenge to the goodness of the world. SEVEN's continuous positive planning for action is distinct from the extremes which lie beyond the wings – FIVE, which contemplates more than it acts, and NINE, which engages naturally in the immediate present without such a complex future plan.

Three in a row

For each individual, home base and its two wings are the three most accessible strategies. Some people use all three of these strategies almost equally. Others depend almost entirely on home base alone.

For the majority, home base remains the usual strategy, and the wings are there as alternatives when required. Often one wing will be used more than the other – but both wings will always be evident to some degree: nobody is trapped completely in the caricature of just one sector of the board.

The wings can be significant in the process of identifying someone's home base. You are looking for "three in a row": home base and the two wings.

If a person appears to show one wing but not the other – only "two in a row" – it may be that what you thought was a wing is actually home base.

Suppose a person showed a lot of NINE and some of EIGHT – but nothing of ONE. Is there perhaps something of SEVEN?

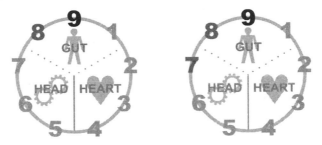

If so, that person is likely to be a natural EIGHT using wing strategy NINE a lot of the time – perhaps even most of the time, for whatever reason.

This becomes more important when we go on to consider the most common moves across the board – because moves are always made from home base, not from a wing.

For yourself, the wings identify your own next closest temptations and spiritual gifts after those of home base. They form part of the map of your potential temptations and gifts – and they invite you to take their paths to redemption: to avoid those temptations and to find those gifts.

A chosen wing

Sometimes people do make long-term use of one of their alternative strategies – in preference, for a while, to the strategy of home base.

Particularly in complex situations – like a complicated extended family or a workplace full of "office politics" – people sometimes consciously choose to take on a new role, to adopt a different approach. They might choose to be, for example – in strategy board numerical order – the person who is always on their best behavior, or the universal carer, or the best in the group, or the moody bohemian, or the silent observer and careful planner, or the perfect group loyalist, or the class clown, or the fighter and protector, or the one who just goes with the flow.

You will know them as this type. They made their choice at some point because, for whatever reason, their usual strategy did not seem to be working – so they consciously decided to adopt a different strategy. They almost certainly picked an alternative strategy that seemed to be within their reach: they almost certainly picked one of their wings.

If someone's type seems just a little too obvious, just a little too much of a caricature, just a little forced, perhaps – then it may well not be their type at all but one of their wings.

And they are likely to be quite unhappy there, in that false adopted role.

Three influential sectors in a row will identify the real home base – and it is there that each person's best gifts and true vocation will be found.

Salvation in the wings

The gifts and temptations of home base, and the gifts and temptations of its two wings, all emerge from similar combinations of head and heart and gut influences – the origin of the "wings" phenomenon. Superficially they can be very different – but their shared origins mean that they can interact in powerful ways. The gifts in the wings can "come to the rescue" – "salvation in the wings" – while the temptations in the wings can all too easily lead to a fall.

For NINE, for example, the temptation toward idleness can be overcome by the idealism at ONE and by the world-challenging determination at EIGHT. The idealism and the challenging determination can also enhance NINE's own natural gifts of peacemaking and reconciliation. But NINE needs to avoid having the temptation toward idleness enhanced by the temptations toward arrogance at EIGHT and anger at ONE.

In the same way, ONE's descent into a perfectionist's anger can be averted by the calmness of NINE and the compassion of TWO. The calmness and the compassion can also enhance ONE's own natural gifts of patience and idealism. ONE just needs to avoid having anger enhanced by obstinacy at NINE or pride at TWO.

TWO's descent into pride can be averted by the idealistic integrity of ONE and the broadly focused gentleness of THREE – both of which can also enhance TWO's own gifts of a self-giving generosity. TWO just needs to avoid the potential judgmentalism of ONE and competitiveness of THREE, either of which could enhance TWO's own temptation toward a self-important pride.

THREE's temptation is a self-protective and competitive deceit. Waiting in the wings are the self-giving of TWO and the creative sensitivity of FOUR – both of which can help THREE to avoid that temptation, and instead develop THREE's gifts of gentleness and hope and inspiration – although THREE needs to avoid letting the pride of TWO or the envy of FOUR add to the original temptation.

FOUR can be tempted to withdraw from the world – but waiting in the THREE wing are gifts for relating to and enriching the lives of others. FOUR can be tempted to look at the world with envy – but waiting in the FIVE wing is a more objective view of the lives that other people live. The gifts in the wings can even help develop FOUR's own gift of creativity – potentially a gift to inspire others, and containing seeds of wisdom. FOUR only needs to avoid having its temptation toward envy compounded instead by THREE's temptation for making a false self-presentation to the world, or FIVE's temptation toward isolation and hoarding.

FIVE can find encouragement to engage with the world – sharing accumulated wisdom rather than withdrawing from the world – in FOUR's heart-influenced creativity and empathy, and in the steady loyal group faithfulness of SIX – carefully avoiding the envy of FOUR and the cowardice of SIX, which might instead enhance the tendency to isolation.

The cowardice of SIX can be overcome, and the loyal faithfulness of SIX enhanced, by calling on the objective discerning wisdom of FIVE, and the brightness and joy of SEVEN – while taking care to avoid the isolation or stinginess of FIVE and the occasional recklessness of SEVEN, both of which may serve as covers for SIXish fear.

SEVEN's excess can be avoided by the steadiness of SIX – and SEVEN's assertion of joy in the face of pain can be enhanced by the assertiveness of EIGHT. SEVEN only needs to avoid the temptations in the wings: SIXish cowardice encouraging SEVEN to hide in a fog of excess, or EIGHTish arrogance and aggression encouraging SEVEN to challenge the world with offensive excess instead of SEVEN's real challenge – which is defeating pain with assertive thanksgiving and positive choices.

And finally EIGHT's temptation to arrogance can be deflated by finding the calmness of NINE and the good humor of SEVEN, opening up a way to work for justice and fairness – ideally without the stubbornness of NINE or the excess of SEVEN along the way.

Moves across the board

Each sector on the strategy board is defined by a particular balance of influences from head and heart and gut. Minor adjustments in that balance give access to the wings – but the wings are always "within reach," right there beside you: they do not involve moving away from home base.

There are situations in which the balance of head and heart and gut can change in a far more significant way. Such a change would represent a move across the board to another sector altogether.

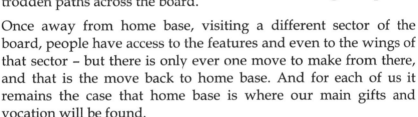

And these moves tend to follow well-trodden paths across the board.

Once away from home base, visiting a different sector of the board, people have access to the features and even to the wings of that sector – but there is only ever one move to make from there, and that is the move back to home base. And for each of us it remains the case that home base is where our main gifts and vocation will be found.

For each of the nine types, there are two "well-trodden paths across the board": the path to the stress type and the path to the security type – the stress move and the security move. And there is a logic about both moves which is – inevitably – all about the balance of head and heart and gut.

Security and stress

The stress type and the security type are the places you might go following particular life events or in particular situations. You might spend half an hour there – or you might spend a decade or more.

The security type is where you tend to go when you feel secure – when life is good.

The stress type is where you tend to go when life is stressful – when the pressure is on.

And then when things get really bad, it may be back to the security type – only this time it is not for feeling secure, but for "clinging to false security".

good times
security type
"feeling secure"

When life is good, you can move to your security type and thrive – showing all its best aspects. You are within easy reach of its spiritual gifts – and its temptations are also close at hand if you become too comfortable there.

regular times
home base

In regular times, you live in your home base sector. You pursue your life journey from corruption toward redemption. Here are the temptations you have lived with day by day for years. Here also is your main calling and vocation – in your home base sector's spiritual gifts.

stressed times
stress type
"thriving under pressure"
"struggling under pressure"

When the pressure is on, you can find yourself in your stress type – possibly "thriving under pressure" in its positive aspects, but also in danger of falling into some of its negative aspects, "struggling under pressure." Life is often stressful, so it makes sense to understand your stress type, and its influence on you through difficult hours, or difficult days, or difficult weeks, or difficult years. You will often be facing its temptations, so you might as well make the most of being there by taking its path to redemption and claiming its spiritual gifts – "redeeming" your stress type.

bad times
security type
"clinging to false security"

And finally, when the pressure is really is on, it's back to the security type – only this time it may not be to its best aspects but to some of its worst aspects and to the trap of its temptation. As life will take you in and out of this sector as well, it makes sense to "redeem" it: to take its path to redemption, dealing with its temptations, and claiming its gifts.

As we work through the stress and security types, revealing these very specific well-trodden paths across the board, you may understand for the first time some of what happens to you to change you so much in different situations – or even how and why you changed in the past, perhaps for decades at a time. And once again, it may help you to understand the people around you: the people they become when life is good, and the very different people they may become when the pressure is on.

Moves for THREE and SIX and NINE

We all use all three resources in varying degrees: head and heart and gut.

For some people, just one resource dominates as they meet each new situation. These are the people at the center of each zone – at THREE and SIX and NINE. For these types, one resource takes the lead, and the other two resources are kept equally "in reserve."

And the two "reserve" resources are indeed there, "in reserve," when required.

Choosing – for whatever reason – to use them, these three types – THREE and SIX and NINE – retain the principle of using just one center at a time. You can almost hear them deciding, in different situations, "I'll go with my head on this one," or "I'll go with my heart on this one," or "I'll go with my gut on this one."

The THREE-SIX-NINE triangle

For their stress and security moves across the board, THREE and SIX and NINE go from the center of one zone to the center of another: they move between THREE and SIX and NINE.

The THREE-SIX-NINE triangle becomes a triangle of well-trodden paths across the board.

The stress move is an anti-clockwise shift, and the security move is a clockwise shift.

By convention, the arrows point in the direction of the stress moves. Security moves go against the arrows.

The shift can reveal itself in countless different ways. These are just a few examples.

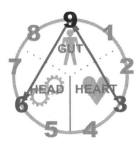

**NINE has
security type THREE
and stress type SIX**

Popular, directly engaging, easy-going NINE, finding NINE's energy and confidence, may emerge as an inspiration and a leader and an achiever – a move to the security type, THREE.

When the pressure is on, and "easy-going" does not seem to be working, NINE may choose an alternative "keep it simple" strategy, which is to stick with the familiar: a move to the stress type, SIX. This could be "thriving under pressure," with SIX emerging positively as confidence and commitment, or it could be struggling under pressure, with SIX emerging negatively as narrowness and intolerance.

When the pressure is really on, NINE may decide that it is time to cheat or compete a way out of the situation in the vicious struggle to survive – the negative side of the security type, THREE.

**THREE has
security type SIX
and stress type NINE**

Leading and achieving THREE, when feeling secure, will be happy just to be a faithful and loyal member of the team – an aspect of the security type, SIX.

When the pressure is on for the team, team leader THREE may become the one who brings peace to the team, and reconciliation if it is needed – "thriving under pressure" at NINE.

Alternatively, when the group dynamics get too complex, THREE may become quite unable to function at all, and just freeze – another aspect of the stress type, NINE.

And when the pressure is really on, prominent THREE may long for nothing more than the chance to become an invisible member of the team, with someone else at the helm: another aspect of the security type, SIX.

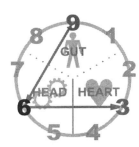

**SIX has
security type NINE
and stress type THREE**

Team member SIXes, when relaxed and secure, can feel quite at home in their environment, freed from the need to be constantly re-evaluating the options, peacefully engaging with their familiar context – a move to the security type, NINE.

SIX's loyalty and faithfulness to the team can encourage SIX to emerge as a heroic team leader when the pressure is on for the team; alternatively, when the pressure is on, SIX may forget the loyalty and compete instead: both are aspects of the stress type, THREE.

And it is only when the pressure is really on that steady SIX would become unable to function or plan, clinging to the idea of taking just one day at time – "keeping it simple" back at the security type, NINE.

Moves for the remaining types

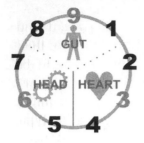

For the remaining six types on the board, the home base strategy emerges from an interaction between a primary influence – which is head or heart or gut – and a secondary influence, which is another of the three.

This pattern is maintained when these types make their stress and security moves: they move from a home base where two resources interact to another sector where two resources interact. THREE and SIX and NINE created a "closed system" of stress and security moves for the three types which have only a primary influence: now the remaining six types – ONE and TWO and FOUR and FIVE and SEVEN and EIGHT – create a "closed system" of stress and security moves for the sectors where there is interaction between a primary and a secondary influence.

Two factors dictate the detail of the moves for these six types: the original conflict between head and heart, and the distance from the gut zone.

Up and down the two sides of the board

The first four major paths for these types enable moves up and down the board – toward and away from the gut zone – without ever crossing that central divide between the head side and the heart side.

On the head side, SEVEN and EIGHT are both head-gut combinations – the logic and reason of the head zone interacting with the direct engagement of the gut zone.

FIVE, also on the head side, is far away from the gut zone, down at the foot of the board.

It is down to FIVE that SEVEN and EIGHT will go when they take a break, for whatever reason, from the direct engagement with the world, which is implied by their contact with the gut zone. They stay on the head side, but move down to the foot of the board, right away from the gut zone, deep into the head zone. FIVE is the natural place of rest and retreat for SEVEN and EIGHT.

And it is to SEVEN and EIGHT that FIVE can go when FIVE determines to move out into the world and engage with it. FIVE stays on the head side, but moves up the board to SEVEN or EIGHT – where head and gut can interact.

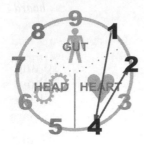

In exactly the same way on the heart side, ONE and TWO are both heart-gut combinations – the emotions and dreams of the heart zone interacting with the direct engagement of the gut zone.

FOUR, also on the heart side, is far away from the gut zone, down at the foot of the board.

It is down to FOUR that ONE and TWO will go when they take a break, for whatever reason, from the direct engagement with the world, which is implied by their contact with the gut zone. They stay on the heart side, but move down to the foot of the board, right away from the gut zone, deep into the heart zone. FOUR is the natural place of rest and retreat for ONE and TWO.

And it is to ONE and TWO that FOUR can go when FOUR determines to move out into the world and engage with it. FOUR stays on the heart side, but moves up the board to a place where heart and gut can interact.

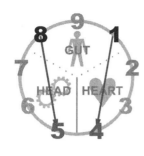

For EIGHT and ONE, in the gut zone itself, the retreat to FIVE or FOUR is the stress move. Under pressure, EIGHT and ONE retreat to a place where they can ponder what is going on. They move as far as possible from the gut zone, but stay on their own side of the head-heart divide: EIGHT goes to FIVE, and ONE goes to FOUR. Thriving under pressure or struggling under pressure, perfectionist-idealist ONE discovers a more deeply emotional, possibly creative side; and fighter-protector EIGHT finds a place to do some thinking, and perhaps find great wisdom.

For SEVEN and TWO, already in the head zone and the heart zone respectively, the move to FIVE or FOUR is the security move.

Feeling secure, head type SEVEN and heart type TWO can find a full flourishing of their respective head or heart main influence in the move to the foot of the board. Relentlessly active SEVEN takes time for relaxation and reflection at FIVE. Giving and caring TWO finds a place of rest and retreat where the self can be nourished a little and where pain can be transformed into beauty and creativity – at FOUR.

The security move is also the move under extreme pressure: over-burdened TWO may withdraw into melancholy at FOUR, and over-active SEVEN may withdraw into hiding at FIVE – but even this move gives to each the opportunity to spend time away from their usual stressful engagements with the world, and hopefully to find refreshment in that rest.

For SEVEN and EIGHT – the head-gut combinations – FIVE is not just "deep in the head zone": it is also in touch with the inner life of the heart, as its secondary influence. Their retreat deep in the head zone becomes a place where SEVEN and EIGHT can also develop the inner life of the heart.

And for ONE and TWO – the heart-gut combinations – FOUR is not just "deep in the heart zone": it is also in touch with the inner life of the head, as its secondary influence. FOUR becomes a place where ONE and TWO can make contact with the key resources of the head zone.

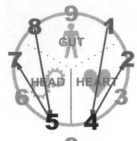

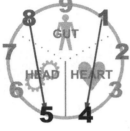

For FIVE and FOUR, the stress and the security moves stay on the same side of the board – but move out toward the gut zone. Both moves are moves outward from the inner life toward direct engagement with the world – without crossing that head-heart divide.

It is the confident security move that takes FIVE and FOUR all the way out to the gut zone itself: FIVE goes to EIGHT and FOUR goes to ONE. Feeling secure, deep-thinking FIVE can come out fighting, at EIGHT. And creative FOUR may find a vision that is ready to engage with the world at ONE – perhaps producing well-finished artworks, or sometimes producing political idealism: the worlds of the artist at FOUR and the idealist at ONE have often overlapped in political history.

The stress moves for FIVE and FOUR are less confident, shorter moves, only to the gut zone boundary of their own familiar sector: FIVE goes to SEVEN and FOUR goes to TWO. Thriving under pressure or struggling under pressure, FIVE applies accumulated wisdom to the task of staying contented and keeping going even though the pressure is on, at SEVEN; and FOUR's deep feeling for the world emerges as practical emotional engagement, one-to-one, with the people around, at TWO. Both FIVE and FOUR stay in their own home zone.

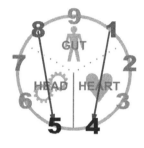

And when the pressure is really on – time for "clinging to false security" – FIVE may once again come out fighting at EIGHT, and FOUR might become harshly judgmental at ONE, against a world that seems so distant and lacking in beauty. Hopefully even these negative experiences of the gut zone will resolve as valuable experience when the pressure eases, and balance is restored, and FIVE and FOUR can reflect once again.

Crossing the top of the board

The moves up and down the two sides of the board have covered both the stress and the security moves for FIVE and FOUR, but only one move each for SEVEN and EIGHT and ONE and TWO.

The same determining factors dictate the four remaining moves: the original conflict between head and heart, and the distance from the gut zone.

So far, SEVEN and EIGHT and ONE and TWO all have the option of withdrawing deep into the inner life on their own side of the board.

In these final moves, they get to cross from one side of the board to the other – but the gut zone dominates every move:

the head-gut combinations
   become heart-gut combinations,

and the heart-gut combinations
   become head-gut combinations.

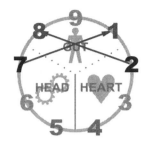

SEVEN and TWO begin any move inside the head zone and the heart zone respectively. The original conflict between head and heart makes it difficult for them to move from one of these zones to the other. Feeling secure, they withdrew away from the gut zone, and flourished deeper in their own zones at FIVE and FOUR respectively – or else hid there, "clinging to false security." For their stress moves – thriving under pressure or struggling under pressure – SEVEN and TWO actually become more engaged with the outside world, not less – moving into the gut zone itself, and at the same time reaching out for the resources of the opposite side of the board: SEVEN goes to ONE, and TWO goes to EIGHT. Under pressure, SEVEN may take a perfectionist-idealist approach to SEVEN's usual planning for positive outcomes: the move to ONE. And giving-caring TWO, under pressure, may get confrontational – in a one-to-one relationship or for the sake of a person in need: the move to EIGHT. Neither move goes all the way from the head zone to the heart zone or vice versa, but each makes at least some contact with the other side of the board – out in the gut zone.

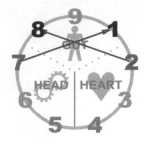

EIGHT and ONE are the gut types with a secondary head or heart influence. Under stress, they withdrew from the gut zone, deep into their secondary influence zones at FIVE and FOUR. In contrast, feeling secure, they have the confidence to go right into the one zone they never usually access – although staying close to their familiar gut zone home: head-side EIGHT goes into the heart zone at TWO, and heart-side ONE goes into the head zone at SEVEN. Feeling secure, the intense idealist ONE relaxes in a playful place at SEVEN, and the fighter-protector EIGHT makes a one-to-one heart connection with the protected at giving and caring TWO.

The security move is also the move under extreme pressure – "clinging to false security." Under extreme pressure, power-conscious and occasionally vengeful EIGHT may hit the worst of patronizing or manipulative TWO. ONE, under extreme pressure, may hide behind a garrulous forced smile at SEVEN, or submit to excess. Hopefully the experience of a new zone will eventually bring enrichment, as things are resolved: there are gifts to be found in every sector, whatever the circumstances that send you there.

In all of this, the original conflict between head and heart has determined every move.

It is the very different gut zone, standing between and alongside the two, which has allowed some limited access from one side to the other.

Apart from the one link in the THREE-SIX-NINE triangle, not a single path crosses that head-heart divide.

Summary of the moves

**EIGHT has
security type TWO
and stress type FIVE**

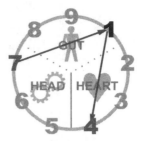

**ONE has
security type SEVEN
and stress type FOUR**

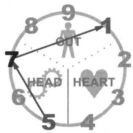

**SEVEN has
security type FIVE
and stress type ONE**

**TWO has
security type FOUR
and stress type TWO**

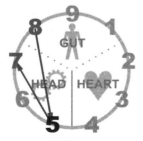

**FIVE has
security type EIGHT
and stress type SEVEN**

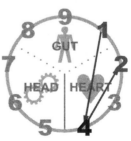

**FOUR has
security type ONE
and stress type TWO**

**NINE has
security type THREE
and stress type SIX**

**SIX has
security type NINE
and stress type THREE**

**THREE has
security type SIX
and stress type NINE**

No better, no worse

To the THREE-SIX-NINE triangle we have added the ONE-FOUR-TWO-EIGHT-FIVE-SEVEN hexagon.

These closed shapes help to emphasize that none of the nine types is any better or any worse than any other. No sector can be condemned as the "bottom of the pit" of stress, and no sector can be lauded as the "pinnacle of achievement" of security: there is potential for good and potential for bad equally in every sector. What matters is what you do when you go there: what you do with that sector's resources and strategy and associated traits. There are temptations and gifts in every sector of the board. And for every type, the main business of life – the real calling and vocation – is the journey from corruption to redemption within the home base sector.

A chosen move

We have already examined the phenomenon of a "chosen" wing. The same thing can happen with stress and security types: people sometimes choose a move.

In some complex situation, someone's usual strategy may appear not to be working – so they consciously choose to take on a different role, to adopt a different approach. This will only work if they choose a strategy that is within their reach. It could be one of their wings, as noted above – or it could be a move across the board to their stress type or their security type. And they could spend decades there.

As with a chosen wing, if someone's type seems just a little too obvious, just a little too much of a caricature, just a little too artificial or forced, then it may well not be their true type at all but their stress type or their security type. Once again, they are likely to be quite unhappy there, in that false adopted role – at least once its temporary purpose has expired, and they find themselves a long way from home, unsure what to do next.

The easy challenge is to stay put and try to "redeem" the chosen type, but this is not a long-term solution. The greater challenge is to find a way back home, there to face the home base temptations, and there to reclaim the original calling and vocation – the gifts of home base.

Life on the axis

Some people end up living not so much in one sector as on one of the nine paths across the board.

Particularly after many years lived in a chosen type – or many decades, not by choice, at the stress or security type – people may find their way home, but still maintain permanent access to the best gifts, and the occasional temptations, of the sector where they spent so very many years.

As just one example from many possibilities, a fighter-protector EIGHT may decide at some point that it is best to leave fighting behind for a while, and go to EIGHT's contemplative stress type FIVE, perhaps for many years. Years later, this "chosen" FIVE finds the personal sense of security to rediscover the directly engaged fighter-protector EIGHT within, and goes home to EIGHT – but this EIGHT never loses the accumulated wisdom and other gifts of those years spent at FIVE, or the occasional twinges of FIVE's temptation, to hoard. Life's journey has left this EIGHT with easy access to all the aspects of sectors EIGHT and FIVE. Home base is EIGHT, but life is lived on the EIGHT-FIVE axis.

Lost FOURs and false TWOs

Contemporary western society is full of "lost FOURs" and "false TWOs."

Our culture does not place a high value on the gifts of FOUR or encourage its vocation. While we like to have creativity and beauty available as commodities – on sale in the shops as required – we do not generally encourage our own to become artists and poets.

As a result, we are surrounded by "lost FOURs" – people whose natural gifts would be at FOUR, but who are living out their lives in some other role.

Some FOURs make it through and live their lives at FOUR – but the lost FOURs take refuge in FOUR's alternative strategies: the wings and the stress and security types.

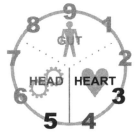

"Lost FOURs" may live mostly in the wings at FIVE or THREE...

Our society does "allow" FIVE – providing various niches for the wise and quiet bookish type – and it positively encourages the popular motivating THREE. Some lost FOURs will take refuge in these "acceptable" roles, which are on FOUR's wings. If you see the quest for understanding of observer FIVE, but none of the easy contentment of group-member SIX, it may be a case of lost FOUR. Is there something, perhaps, of heart-zone THREE? And if you see THREE's heart-zone gift of inspiring others combined not so much with the one-to-one engagement of TWO but with a quieter observing thoughtfulness – an aspect of FIVE – it may again be a case of lost FOUR.

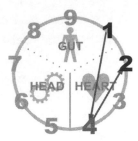

...or at the stress and security types ONE and TWO

Other lost FOURs take refuge in FOUR's stress and security types, living out their lives at ONE and TWO. People whose FOURish gifts would otherwise lead them into the arts, end up at ONE as engineers or solicitors or accountants or pharmacists, or at TWO in "the caring professions." They sometimes find their way home later in life, surprising people with an apparently new interest in music or painting or furniture restoration or local history or genealogy or creative writing. If somebody seems to be all ONE and TWO, they could well be "lost FOUR" – and FOUR is where their most natural gifts will be found.

The phenomenon of "the lost FOURs" emerges from the expectations of contemporary western society. These expectations are changing in subtle ways all the time – but an enduring feature is that they often differ according to gender. Society at large is more ready to allow to women than to men a FOURish artistic and creative side – but more than anything, it expects of women a TWOish giving and caring role, in the home and beyond. Many women are pushed by the pressures around them into assuming only this giving and caring role, even when their real gifts lie elsewhere. These are the "false TWOs."

"False TWOs" may be ONEs or THREEs living in the TWO wing...

The real home base of "false TWO" may be idealistic ONE, with wings NINE and TWO, or inspirational THREE, with wings TWO and FOUR – but they are pushed into living life entirely in the TWO wing, as "false TWO."

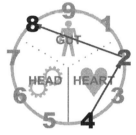

...or EIGHTs or FOURs who have made the stress or security move to TWO

Or the real home base may be a strong and challenging EIGHT or – inevitably – a creative FOUR: but they are pushed to their stress or security point to live life as "false TWO."

Parenthood rightly demands immeasurable amounts of giving and caring – a task best shared by both parents but too often left to the mother. It can be a wonderful liberation later in life for a role-bound "false TWO" to begin to rediscover their other natural gifts and the rest of their vocation at their natural home base – whatever that may be.

There are other "false" and "lost" phenomena. Western society has historically defined confrontational EIGHT as a "masculine" role, as well as defining caring TWO as a "feminine" role: indeed all the types could be ranked by different degrees of artificial gender stereotyping.

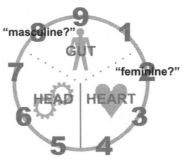

The reality is that the resources of head and heart and gut are distributed without regard to gender. All that the culture has achieved with its stereotyping is to create the further classes of female "lost EIGHTs" and male "lost TWOs" and so on – all of whom will rejoice to find their way home.

More recently, strong women at EIGHT and caring men at TWO have become celebrated icons of contemporary culture – distinctive in comparison to the assumptions of the past, but lauded and applauded in the "post-feminist" present.

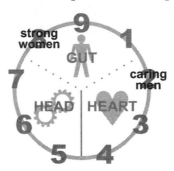

In the end, any culture – or any micro-culture like a household or a workplace or a church – can force whole classes of people into trying to be what they are not. Depending on the time and the place and the reason, people can end up living in a role that neglects or even denies their real gifts. The journey back to home base may be painful and stressful in many ways, but it is back at home base that each person will ultimately find their best gifts and their true vocation.

Access all areas

**THREE and SIX and NINE
have access to all sectors**

For five of the nine types, the moves and the wings combine to give at least some access to every sector of the board.

Everyone on the THREE-SIX-NINE triangle, for example, has at least some access to all nine sectors of the board – through the three types on the triangle itself, and then through the wings of each of those types.

The other two types with this access to "all areas" are the remaining gut types, EIGHT and ONE – again by adding together home base, the stress move, the security move, and the wings of all three.

Typically, it is the distinctive gut zone which best allows access to the whole board – the whole of the head side and the whole of the heart side.

**Gut type EIGHT
has access to all sectors**

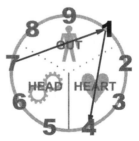

**Gut type ONE
has access to all sectors**

For the remaining types – SEVEN and FIVE and FOUR and TWO – the situation is less straightforward, highlighting once again the fundamental contrast between head and heart.

**Head type SEVEN
lacks access
to heart sector THREE**

Adding together the wings, and the moves, and the wings of the moves, SEVEN has access to the whole of the head zone and the whole of the gut zone – but in the heart zone only touches TWO and FOUR as the wings of ONE and FIVE. Positive SEVEN has many gifts, but with no easy access to THREE; SEVEN does not easily make a natural leader or a competitive achiever.

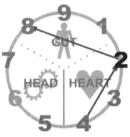

**Heart type TWO
lacks access
to head sector SIX**

The same logic applies for heart type TWO, the mirror image of SEVEN. Involved compassionate TWO – responding to every need – can take on many roles, but the low-profile group membership of head type SIX is perhaps the least accessible.

Furthest of all from the gut zone, FIVE and FOUR have the least access of all from one side of the board to the other. Their stress and security moves give full access to their own side of the board – but even with the wings added in, the only access across that central divide is deep in the inner life where FIVE and FOUR meet as head and heart wings of each other.

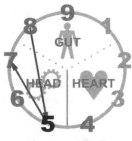

Head type FIVE lacks access to sectors ONE and TWO and THREE

Head type FIVE has no easy access to heart side sectors ONE and TWO and THREE. Observer FIVE may take on many roles, but the least accessible are perhaps impulsive ONE, emotionally involved TWO, and the effortless mastery of group dynamics at THREE. SIX and SEVEN and EIGHT and NINE all provide ways for FIVE to relate to others – but the real relating of the heart, for FIVE, is always in that most profound place, deep in the heart zone at FOUR.

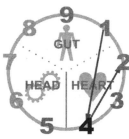

Heart type FOUR lacks access to sectors EIGHT and SEVEN and SIX

The same logic applies for FIVE's symmetrical opposite, heart type FOUR, which has no easy access to head-side sectors EIGHT and SEVEN and SIX. The creative individualist that is FOUR may take on many roles, but the least accessible are perhaps thick-skinned EIGHT, happy-go-lucky SEVEN, and contented low-profile group member SIX. And when FOUR wants to observe and reason – making use of the head zone resources – it will always be with that detached objectivity of FIVE – the one place where FOUR touches the head zone.

Longing for the opposite

We all have gifts and talents and abilities built into our home base sector – but we all long for more gifts, more talents, more abilities. Perhaps we long most consciously for those that would most complement or balance the ones we have – the very gifts and talents and abilities that are least like our own.

Those are the gifts and talents and abilities that are diametrically opposite our own on the strategy board – in those sectors of the board where our own natural balance of head and heart and gut is completely reversed. We long for the opposites – and the opposites become "the wannabe types."

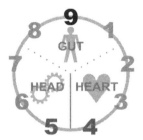 

NINEs, who live continuously in the present tense, long for FIVE's ability to find some distance and objective wisdom, and for FOUR's ability to find an imaginative richness and creativity – both of which are to be found in a place of quiet separation from the immediate.

NINE may find some access to the gifts of FIVE and FOUR through the wings of the stress and security types SIX and THREE.

THREEs, forever changing to suit the mood of the audience, might wish they could more easily stand up against the crowd for a principle, like EIGHTs. Stressed at times by the complexities of managing group dynamics from the heart, they might also long for the simple, less emotionally involved happiness of SEVENs.

THREE may find some access to the gifts of EIGHT and SEVEN through the wings of the stress and security types NINE and SIX.

SIXes may look with envy at the passion in TWOs' relationships compared to the headish logic of their own – and may also look with envy at ONEs who have such energy and passion in believing and promoting the ideals and standards within which SIX chooses quietly to live.

SIX may find some access to the gifts of TWO and ONE through the wings of the stress and security types THREE and NINE.

EIGHTs, forever challenging and fighting, might wish that instead they could communicate profoundly like FOUR, or lead naturally and effortlessly like THREE.

EIGHT may find some access to the gifts of FOUR and THREE through the wings of the stress and security types FIVE and TWO.

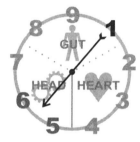 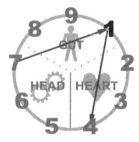

ONEs can be exhausted and half destroyed by their own perfectionism and their fight against all that is less than ideal. They may look with envy at the ease with which SIXes live good lives in the world just as it is – and long also for the calm, detached, and objective wisdom of FIVE.

ONE may find some access to the gifts of FIVE and SIX through the wings of the stress and security types FOUR and SEVEN.

 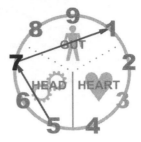

SEVENs, carefully planning the day ahead and managing their friendships in the head, might long for the instant heart connections that seem to come so easily in friendships for TWO and in groups for THREE.

Head zone SEVEN may find some access to the gifts of TWO on the wing of stress type ONE – but lacks easy access to the gifts of THREE right in the middle of the heart zone.

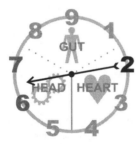 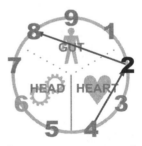

TWOs, drained by their emotional engagements with others, might look jealously at SEVENs with their constantly cheerful friendships – and at the simple lives of SIXes who seem to fit in so easily and play their full part with so much less emotional cost.

Heart zone TWO may find some access to the gifts of SEVEN on the wing of stress type EIGHT – but lacks easy access to the gifts of SIX right in the middle of the head zone.

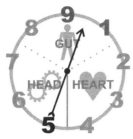 

FIVEs may admire ONE's ability to engage with the world so directly and so passionately – and also look to NINEs, who live full and engaged lives without the constant noise and complexity of FIVE's endlessly churning mind.

FIVE may find some access to the gifts of NINE on the wing of security type EIGHT, but lacks easy access to the gifts of ONE – out there in the gut zone, and on the other side of the board as well.

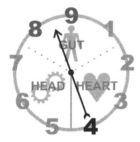 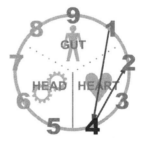

And from their place of deep emotions and their sense of distance from the world, FOURs look with envy at NINE's ability to engage with the world so directly while maintaining an easy sense of peace and calmness and innocence – and also at EIGHT's engaged ability to challenge.

FOUR may find some access to the gifts of NINE on the wing of security type one, but lacks easy access to the gifts of EIGHT – out there in the gut zone, and on the other side of the board as well.

We saw in Part 1 that taking the advice of the opposites can be part of the path to redemption for everyone – so that "longing for the opposite" has a purpose. Emulating the opposite may not come naturally – FOUR will never be a natural fighter-protector like EIGHT – but there will always be situations where the advice of the opposites will be the best advice. We do all have at least something of all three resources – of head and heart and gut – and while it might not come naturally, sometimes we just need to pull them together in the combination that the best advice demands, and do what we can.

Colleagues of the opposite type

Of course you only want to be the best of your "wannabe" type – your opposite. Your attitude toward the negative side of the sectors opposite your own may well be slightly superior: that you know you're not that, and you're glad you're not that.

As a result, you may see no role at all for a colleague who displays the negative side of your "opposite" – but a colleague showing the best side of your opposite may be the most valuable colleague of all.

Colleagues from diametrically opposite sides of the board may never really understand each other, and may work slightly awkwardly around each other, but they can be full of admiration and respect for each other, and they make a superb complementary team.

On the basis that the advice of the opposite is often good advice, you may find that the colleague you understand the least is often the best person to ask for advice in a situation where you cannot see a way forward yourself. That "opposite" colleague may well see a clear way forward straight away.

And if all goes well, the compliment may be returned: you may well have immediate and easy access to exactly the advice that your opposite needs when their usual approach cannot see any way forward.

This "complementarity of the opposite" may be difficult to manage from day to day – but it can be highly productive in the longer term.

Discerning home base – Part 2

Discerning home base can be a complex process.

Choices being made "live," "right now," may be influenced not only by an individual's current place on the board, but also by the two wings of the current place on the board.

And the current place on the board may be home base – or it may be the stress type, or it may be the security type.

The full life story of "who I am" will include stories of time spent elsewhere on the board in the past – and the influence of those times on the present.

And longing for the opposites can become such a significant part of a person's self-image that they may claim more affinity with the opposites than with home base – against which they "rebel."

To identify home base correctly is to identify not just one significant sector, but this whole pattern of wings and moves and opposites – and in the infinite diversity of humankind, the details of the pattern will be unique to each individual.

Each individual will have a unique life history of time spent at different places on the board – at home base and in the stress and security sectors. The frequency and timing of the moves – in hours or in decades – will be unique. The reasons for the moves, and the experience gained, will be unique.

Each individual will have a unique way of relating to the opposites: the advice of the opposites, the temptations and gifts of the opposites, and colleagues or acquaintances of the opposite types.

And the experience of home base and its wings will be unique to each individual. There will always be at least some experience of all three sectors – home base and the two wings – but each individual establishes their own unique mix of characteristics from the three. They can be used in almost any combination: all three strongly, any two of the three strongly, or any one of the three dominating – although the best gifts and the true vocation and the sense of home will only ever be found at home base.

The process of discerning home base involves identifying a whole pattern of influential sectors – in which the key elements are generally home base, its two wings, the stress type and the security type.

The relative strengths of these five can vary greatly – and home base is not always the most obvious. There are "lost FOURs" and "false TWOs" and the rest. "Chosen wings" and "chosen moves" cry out for attention – often louder than home base. And some sectors – often the opposites – will be more "desired" than actually influential. Identifying a whole pattern of influential sectors can be essential in determining which one among them is the true home base.

Within that pattern, the various influential sectors will not be experienced as "neutrally interchangeable." Being at home base and using the home base strategy is a very different experience from being "away from home" in the stress or security sector or using the strategy of one of the wings. Part of the process of discerning home base is to consider the various influential sectors in terms of which seem the most natural and which seem more artificial or strained. For each influential sector in turn, it is worth considering whether the individual seems comfortable and at ease with that sector and strategy – or whether it might instead be the result of a conscious choice, or a response to circumstances, or the consequence of security or stress. The home base strategy is "what comes naturally": the rest may have a role, but none will feel like home.

Couples

People use their various strategies when they approach anything new. Sometimes "the new thing" is another person – who will also be using a range of strategies. The various strategies begin to interact – and the result is the infinite variety of human interactions.

From this complexity of interactions, patterns still emerge – and one instructive place to observe them is in one-to-one relationships that become long-term stable partnerships.

All kinds of long-term stable partnerships are possible, and they all have their own unique dynamics – but in contemporary western culture, the most common form to emerge by far is between two people of adjacent types: two people with neighboring home bases.

This "adjacent pairs" phenomenon is especially evident in couples who meet in their late teens or in their twenties. In contemporary western culture, young adults in particular have a certain set of assumptions about the intimacy, compatibility, and complementarity they expect to find in a one-to-one relationship. "Romantic bonding" of this particular youthful and idealistic kind tends to flourish between two people of adjacent types – and this pairing then has a good track record for helping them "stay the course" as a long-term stable partnership.

The "adjacent pairs" phenomenon is all about balancing compatibility with complementarity. Two people of the same type could spend too much time stepping on each other's toes – finding it difficult to share the same space, and having relatively little to add to each other's lives. Two people too distant from each other might have too little in common: they may not "understand" each other; they might not make that "special connection." Adjacent types appear to be "the perfect match" for creating a strong and intimate bond that can nourish both partners – balancing compatibility with complementarity.

The "adjacent pairs" phenomenon is so common that it becomes a powerful tool in helping to discern someone's type. If you know two people in a long-term stable partnership – especially one founded in young adulthood in our contemporary western culture – you almost certainly have two people of adjacent types: you have a ONE-TWO couple, or a TWO-THREE couple, or a THREE-FOUR couple, or a FOUR-FIVE couple, or a FIVE-SIX couple, or a SIX-SEVEN couple, or a SEVEN-EIGHT couple, or an EIGHT-NINE couple, or a NINE-ONE couple. As with just one person, you have nine possibilities – but with two people in the partnership, you have twice as many clues.

No relationship is entirely straightforward – and there are two great ways for "adjacent pair" couples to row. One is to swap places – not difficult as each partner's type is a wing of the other's. Each leans over so far to see the other's point of view on some issue that they actually pass each other and swap places. Each feels very generous for taking a stance according to the other's usual priorities, and so is greatly frustrated to find that the other now seems to have moved. The other great way to row is for each partner to move to the wing the other partner does not share. This leaves the couple a long way apart, and almost certainly unable to communicate – unable to understand each other. Recognizing in each case that this is what is going on can make it all much less frightening – and much easier to avoid.

One of the confident assertions of contemporary culture is that it is always good to talk things through. This may well be true in structured organizations, governed according to logical written rules – but it will often not be true for an "adjacent pair" couple. Unless they are both in the head zone – the home of logic and words – the best solution is often to say nothing at all. Heart types and gut types are reconciled more easily by a kiss and an embrace and a bit of romance – because words are not the way that they communicate. An excellent piece of alternative advice is this classic: "when you are wrong, say so; when you are right, say nothing." Of course, if two people as a couple really have lost their way, it may help to have some assisted rational head type analysis of what is going on – in their heads, and in their hearts, and in their gut reactions – but day by day outside the head zone, most communication happens in different ways.

Finally on the "adjacent pairs": some relationships flounder because people meet, apparently as adjacent types, when one of them is actually away from home base at their stress or security point. After what seems like a perfectly stable beginning, one partner seems to pull away from all that the couple held in common. It's that break-up cliché – "I needed to find myself" – and that is exactly what the person is doing: leaving the stress or security point, and therefore the basis of the relationship, and going on a journey to find home base again. It has actually been the relationship that has helped them and resolved the stress – as the person leaving will often testify at the tearful farewell. Other couples who find themselves in this situation eventually learn to understand each other again: for a while, they may seem like strangers to each other, but their lives are intertwined, and years spent at a stress or security point remain a part of who we are: there is always hope and new potential.

There are two other recognizable patterns in long-term stable partnerships – though neither is as common as the "adjacent pair."

The first is the partnership between individuals whose home bases are diametric opposites on the board. Each is one of the other's opposite or "wannabe" types. Individuals in these partnerships are full of admiration for each other, rejoicing in their very difference – their complementarity. Partners meeting later in life often form such partnerships and grow together "in all three zones." There is more of a sense of choice and reflection about forming the relationship – even formality rather than "inevitability" in the choosing – and the couple live and grow together and delight in each other on that basis. There may be times when they do not understand each other, but admiration and generosity and forbearance see them through.

And the other recognizable form of partnership has some features of the "opposites" partnership and some features of the "adjacent pairs" partnership. It is the partnership between individuals whose home bases are at either end of a stress and security path – such as a ONE-SEVEN couple. The shared link along the stress and security path creates features like those in an "adjacent pair" relationship – but the physical distance across the board creates features like those in an "opposites" relationship. The result is often a sparky but very committed relationship: creative, complementary, and admiring – and able to clash and forgive.

There must be many other types of committed partnership out there, but these three do emerge regularly and distinctively in our culture from among the potentially limitless patterns of human interaction.

Colleagues and friends

As for couples, so also for colleagues and friends, and all other relationships: in the infinite variety of human interactions, patterns emerge as individuals using their various strategies meet and interact.

Colleagues of the same type are likely to feel that they are in each other's way, while colleagues from different zones will find – for better or for worse – that they have different perspectives on the same situations.

Three of the most distinctive "colleague relationships" are parallel to those already described for couples – for the same basic reasons. Colleagues of adjacent types may form a robust long-term working partnership: a distinctive blend of mutual understanding and common purpose with a dash of complementarity. Colleagues at either end of a stress and security path may well find that they have quite a sparky interaction, particularly at first – but it may well develop into a creative, complementary, committed, and mutually admiring relationship. And the relationship between colleagues of opposite types is so distinctive that it already has a section of its own above. Colleagues from opposite sides of the board may never really understand each other, and may work slightly awkwardly around each other, but they can be full of admiration and respect for each other, and can make an excellent complementary team.

Long-term friendships also produce the same distinctive patterns. Two people of the same type may find it very easy to understand each other – but find that they each have relatively little to add to each other's experience of life. Two people at the opposite ends of a stress and security path may form a friendship that is creative, complementary, committed, and mutually admiring – but which veers unpredictably between closeness and formality. Mutually admiring opposites may have a more classically formal, respectful acquaintanceship. And the strongest intimate bond is once again between two people of neighboring types.

When you add together the adjacent pairs phenomenon in couples and in friendships, you find couples being friends with other couples to make up groups of four where only adjacent types are represented – whether four adjacent types, or only three, or only two – and the dynamics of the several relationships operate according to the expected interactions of those types.

Age and the journey

Perhaps home base is dictated by our genes, or in the development of our brains before we are born. Perhaps it is a result of our early nurture – or perhaps it emerges from the choices we make when we first encounter the world around us, trying out first one strategy and then another until we find one that seems to work for us in the situations that we face. Whichever way home base is determined, we have probably taken up residence there by the age of five, ready to face the unpredictable world of the early years of school.

The strategy that each person develops and refines over the next ten years – from five to fifteen – is the strategy that will then launch them into the adult world as they go through "coming of age" and into young adulthood. The strategy that they have practiced through the school years is all that they have to rely upon as they suddenly have to apply it "for real" in countless more situations in the adult world.

For many people, their type is most evident – most obvious – if they think about how they were in their twenties.

And it is in their twenties and thirties that people are most likely to feel "stuck in a rut" – locked into a single way of operating and a single mode of living, compared to the great variety of different lives being lived by the people around them. They are living with one particular set of strengths and weaknesses and gifts and temptations, shared with just a small minority of the rest of the world – about one in nine – while all the rest seem to have such a great variety of different and exciting lives.

If we feel it intensely, we may choose to take action: to change, to explore some other aspect of who we are, to grasp some other life which seems to be within our reach – a place excitingly different from the familiar home base, but almost certainly a wing or a stress or security type. On the way, we face new temptations and we make new mistakes, but we also discover new strengths and new gifts, as life and experience are broadened forever.

For most of us, life itself is more than varied enough to ensure that we do not remain stuck in a rut for long. Life provides us with new challenges, which call on us to try out different strategies, and we rise to the challenge, discovering – if we try a wing strategy – that we are good for the task. And then life applies pressure, pushing us over to our stress type, or offers times of great security, drawing us to our security type. Life puts the pressure on hard and drives us over to our security type again. We make these moves around the board, encountering new temptations, facing new challenges, learning as we go, and finding new gifts and potentials that we never knew were there.

Age is a factor. The longer you have played the game, the more you have learned, and seen, and become. More temptations and gifts will have been collected along the way, more paths will have been walked, more challenges overcome. More of your wide potential will have been developed: as well as home base, you are more likely to have well-developed stress and security types, and the wings of all three. The journeys and stories of more sectors – perhaps of all nine – will feel strongly familiar. Others may find it harder to place you, with your accumulated gifts and your breadth of character – but even long into the journey, there is still one sector which is the most peaceful and natural and familiar place. For all the development and balance of character brought by age and experience, it is still possible to identify the gentle lure of home.

The path to redemption – Part 2

In Part 1 we identified the basic "path to redemption" for any sector of the board:

- deal with the temptation
- claim the gift
- make use of all three resources (head and heart and gut)
- take the advice of the opposites

Here in Part 2 we have seen how the wings and the moves give everyone access to a range of sectors in addition to home base – so for the full journey to redemption, we could pluralize the first two items: "deal with the temptations"; "claim the gifts."

But there is more to the wings and the moves than simply the addition of more gifts and temptations. The gifts and temptations in the wings can interact with home base in powerful ways – to compound the temptations or to find "salvation in the wings." And the moves give access to sectors some distance from home base, often bringing valuable experience of other zones and other resources. Whatever the circumstances that send us to the stress or security points, one result is that other resources have been developed. For the long term, the journey toward redemption may well have been advanced as we learn to "make use of all three resources."

So here at the conclusion of Part 2 we have a fuller outline of the "generic" path to redemption. Wherever you are on the board – home sector, stress sector, or security sector:

- deal with the temptations
- claim the gifts
- avoid the temptations in the wings
- develop the gifts in the wings
- use what you have learned elsewhere on the board to make use of all three resources (head and heart and gut)
- take the advice of the opposites

And somewhere on your journey, find your way back home – to recognize, value, and develop the gifts of your home base sector.

They are wonderful gifts with wonderful applications. They are your true calling and vocation – and the place to call home.

Part 3

Biblical Journeys

The biblical heroes

All of the heroes of Scripture are a mixture of human frailty and divine grace. They show us how we, as frail human beings, might also be used by God, for God's purposes. There are biblical examples of all nine types – illustrating once again that God can use us all.

SIX – Peter

We first meet Simon Peter as a fisherman – working in partnership with his brother Andrew.

Fishing is a good classic family business. You learn the ways of the sea – here the Sea of Galilee: its seasons, the workings of the wind and the waves, and how these interact with the fish below the surface day by day and year by year. You learn how to use and preserve the boats and the nets. You are faithful to the life. It is a good classic family business.

It is a great place for SIX. For dependable fishing, you stick with what you know.

Jesus calls both Simon and Andrew – and further along the shoreline, the brothers James and John (Matthew 4:18-22).

These four – and especially Peter, James, and John – become the small central group of Jesus' disciples. They are together at the beginning – the first to be called and involved in Jesus' ministry (Mark 1:29-31) – and they are together near the end: according to Mark, it is to these four only that Jesus speaks, in the few days before the crucifixion, of the tribulations that lie ahead for the disciples (Mark 13:3-13). Peter, James, and John are the chosen three who accompany Jesus at the transfiguration (Mark 9:2), at a controversial healing (Mark 5:35-37), and in Gethsemane (Matthew 26:37). Peter is a loyal companion for Jesus, within this small group: all naturally SIX.

Jesus calls on the gifts of SIX – loyalty and faithfulness – when he grants to Simon Peter the name "the rock": the rock on which Jesus will build the church, the solid rock unmoved even by death and the underworld (Matthew 16:18). And it is to faithful and loyal Simon Peter that Jesus grants "the keys of heaven" and the task of "binding and loosing" in the name of heaven (Matthew 16:19). These are tasks fitting to the best gifts of loyal and faithful SIX.

We see Jesus calling on the gifts of SIX in Peter – but SIX is often full of fear, caught between confidence and cowardice. The confidence is sometimes foolhardy – and sometimes truly faithful and truly courageous: emerging from cover, SIX may confront and overcome its fears by summoning up its confidence in something greater.

Peter steps out of the boat in the storm to walk toward Jesus on the water. It was even his own idea. Then at the sound of the wind he becomes fearful once again and begins to sink. And yet he still trusts in the one he knows – and calls on Jesus to save him (Matthew 14:28-31). The whole episode is a study in the dynamics of SIX.

Peter at the transfiguration is "exceedingly afraid" (Mark 9:6) – but true to SIX, from somewhere inside, Peter remembers some convention about hospitality, so he goes with what he knows – and offers to build booths (Mark 9:2-8).

In the enthusiasm to walk on the water, and in the bizarre offer on the mountain top, we see Peter rising above tremendous fear, not only with faithfulness and loyalty and trust but also with hints of the SEVEN wing: the optimist, and the generalist, rushing in to the point of excess.

It is with more SIX loyalty and courage, and more SEVEN enthusiasm, that Peter alone declares to Jesus: "You are the Christ, the Son of the living God" (Matthew 16:13-16). Peter must have been thinking this through and wondering – making the connections between what he saw in Jesus and what he knew the Messiah was to be: aspects of the FIVE wing in SIX. This declaration also shows Peter thriving under pressure at SIX's stress type THREE – taking an inspirational lead in the group – and yet only moments later Peter is gripped once again by SIX's fear, as Jesus tells of what lies ahead in Jerusalem (Matthew 16:21-22).

We also see the temptation of SIX's stress type THREE when Peter is under pressure: challenged over the small matter of the temple tax, Peter nervously asserts that Jesus pays it – before actually checking with Jesus himself. Later, Jesus addresses the topic rather less conventionally: "the sons of kings do not pay tribute." The SIXish tension is resolved as the tax is paid – using a coin found in a fish (Matthew 17:24-27).

And during the years of Jesus' teaching it is often head type Peter who asks for a logical explanation of a parable or a saying (Matthew 15:15; 19:27) – once again showing the FIVE wing in SIX.

Through the distressing events of Maundy Thursday night – after the arrest of Jesus – Peter once again shows the gifts and temptations of SIX. He is loyal enough to follow Jesus at a distance – but he cowers in the shadows nearby (Matthew 26:58). His denial of Jesus is an act of fear – despite his earlier pledge of loyalty to the point of death (Matthew 26:33,35). As SIX he knows the gravity of what he has done (Matthew 26:69-75). He is taken right back to the sense of utter unworthiness that he has at the beginning ("Depart from me, Lord, for I am a sinful man" – Luke 5:8): Peter is painfully aware of his own transgression.

SIXes grow tall on affirmation and encouragement and attention – affirmation not so much of their individuality as of their membership, their belonging. They do not expect it – as they try to disappear into the crowd – but it makes them thrive when it comes from people they respect, as it helps them to know that they are valued for their contribution. Jesus knows this, continually drawing Peter into the inner group of disciples – and on resurrection morning, the angel by the garden tomb knows this, mentioning Peter by name: "Go, tell his disciples and Peter that he goes before you to Galilee" (Mark 16:7). At the lakeside, the risen Jesus knows it too, and gives Peter the chance to declare his commitment not once but three times – even as Peter is in the middle of giving up on the whole project and returning to what he knows, which is fishing. When Peter sees the risen Jesus waiting for them, he switches his loyalty straight back, and leaps into the sea. In the three-fold declaration of commitment that follows, Peter uses the word for love in Greek, which is the committed, loyal, steadfast, and dependable love of SIX. There, Jesus affirms and commissions him once again: feed my sheep; follow me (John 21:1-17).

Emerging as group leader THREE after the ascension – SIX thriving under pressure – Peter takes the lead in arranging for the appointment of a replacement twelfth apostle, Matthias – although they meekly use the casting of lots to make the final decision, and take corporate responsibility for it (Acts 1:15-26).

Again, on the day of Pentecost, it is Peter who takes the lead – to stand up and speak to the crowds in Jerusalem – but even here he needs to know that the whole group is with him: Acts 2:14 tells us not that Peter stood up alone to address the crowd, but that he stood "with the eleven."

And from that time onward Peter assumes the charge that he has been given – to be at the heart of the team. A confident team member who is a reluctant team leader may become the best team leader of all: thriving under pressure to lead and achieve – and remaining faithful and loyal.

Peter becomes the leader of the church in Rome, not just Jerusalem – but there is one more hurdle along the way. In the comfort of Jerusalem, Peter finds it too easy too often to forget the freedom of the gospel and slip back into the habits of the law. This is SIX, for comfort, clinging to what SIX knows – and also SIX's comfortable security type NINE, taking the path of least resistance for the sake of an easy life. The clash with Paul on this issue is recorded by Paul himself (Galatians 2:11-16) and by Luke – in an account rather more favorable to Peter and James (Acts 15:1-35).

In Peter we see the gifts of SIX well used, the temptations of SIX confronted, the hints of the wings at SEVEN and FIVE, and the stress and security types visited at THREE and at NINE.

And Peter's journey to redemption is SIX's journey, before and after the resurrection: learning to trust God and self a little instead of just those dry old rules; questioning and dismantling some of the old boundaries; learning to trust more, and to fear less. In his early years as the leader of the church in Jerusalem, it could have served Peter well to remember more often the Jesus who was like a perfect loyal friend – who could have fun, laugh a little, and enjoy the richness of life.

THREE – Jacob

There is probably something THREE-SIX-NINE about all twin relationships: not necessarily about each twin, but certainly about the relationship – which at different times has loyalty, and competitiveness, and a comfortable peace.

Jacob is a twin, and Jacob is THREE. Even before he is born he fights with his brother (Genesis 25:22-23). With their father Isaac old and weak, the unredeemed Jacob conspires with his mother Rebekah to deceive Isaac, and cheat his older twin Esau out of their father's blessing (Genesis 27:1-29). This is a very THREE plot – competitive, deceitful – but it also makes slightly manipulative use of his close relationship with his mother Rebekah (Genesis 25:28) – a sub-plot on the unredeemed TWO wing. Jacob is then forced to flee the country to escape his brother's anger, and plans to stay with his uncle, Rebekah's brother Laban (Genesis 27:41-45). This is a very THREE response – fleeing the site of apparent or imminent failure.

Jacob is leaving behind all that he knows. The journey across country is not just a difficult practical journey, but a traumatic symbolic journey as well – a cue for any THREE to touch the FOUR wing, and here it is: on the journey, in a vision, he sees a great mound – an earthwork, not a ladder – with the angels of God ascending and descending upon it. For the culture of the time, heaven was literally up above, and high places were holy places which touched heaven: the vision is a vision of a holy place, "the house of God, the gate of heaven," and there God makes a promise to Jacob that he will be the father of a great nation, and more besides (Genesis 28:10-17). This must have warmed the heart of a fleeing THREE, though it would be decades before any hint of fulfillment.

In the morning, inspired by the dream, Jacob prays for the day when he might return to his father's house in peace (Genesis 28:18-22): feeling the pressure, Jacob touches stress type NINE, which is the place of reconciliation and peace.

In the home of Laban, Jacob works fourteen years for the hands in marriage of his cousins, Laban's daughters, Rachel and Leah (Genesis 29:15-28). He serves those years with loyalty and faithfulness in the welcoming safety of this family home – Jacob at security point SIX.

It is when his chosen Rachel gives birth to her firstborn, Joseph, that Jacob once again dreams of home, and reconciliation (Genesis 30:22-26), but his departure is delayed, and some complex competitiveness and trickery takes place as Jacob and Laban determine what should belong to each of them when Jacob finally departs (Genesis 30:27-43). Relationships are soured (Genesis 31:1-2) and the time has come for Jacob to return to his father's house. He leaves by stealth (Genesis 31:17-21) provoking one final row with Laban (Genesis 31:22-42) but it ends this time with reconciliation (Genesis 31:43-55) and Jacob is free to leave in peace – and face the challenge of approaching his brother.

Jacob is encouraged by another vision of angels (Genesis 32:1-2), and sends a humble message ahead to his brother Esau (Genesis 32:3-5). Nevertheless he is "greatly afraid and distressed," and he pleads with God for deliverance, clinging to the promise of God made two decades before (Genesis 32:6-12). Security point SIX – under this intense pressure – is the origin both of the fear and of the faithful and courageous trust in God's promise.

Clinging – at SIX – to the common convention that gifts show goodwill, Jacob sends gift after gift on ahead of him (Genesis 32:13-21). That night he even sends his beloved family on ahead, and he is left alone with his fear of what the day ahead will bring (Genesis 32:21-23). That night Jacob wrestles alone with a vision until daybreak – and the result is a draw. This is all very FOUR and SIX and THREE: visionary and fearful and competitive all at once. Jacob demands a blessing from his rival, and interprets the vision as a meeting with God. Jacob has spent the night struggling with his past, and with his future – with his place in eternity. Whatever the vision may have been, it was real enough to leave him limping from the fight as the new day began (Genesis 32:24-32). And the next day – the blessing is fulfilled, as Esau receives his brother, and they are reconciled (Genesis 33:1-4) – thriving under pressure at point NINE.

And now Jacob, at last, is in a "redeemed" place, where the best gifts of THREE can begin to emerge. He becomes the team leader for his large family – one daughter, twelve sons – gently trying to keep them all on the straight and narrow, and at peace with one another. As father of the twelve sons, he even becomes team leader for the nation, which bears his name Israel: he was given this name, meaning "strives with God," when he wrestled with the angel – for as the angel said, "You have striven with God and with men, and have prevailed" (Genesis 32:28).

We have seen Jacob, THREE, take his journey to the linked types SIX and NINE.

We have seen his visionary FOUR wing – and we see FOUR again when he presents his favored son Joseph, aged just seventeen, with the famous long sleeved robe (Genesis 37:3).

We see the TWO wing in Jacob's close relationship with his own mother Rebekah, and in his special compassion for Rachel and Joseph, and later for Benjamin (Genesis 29:18; 37:3; 42:4). And we see TWO again as Jacob now seeks to "mother" his own children and watch over his family, however imperfectly that may be.

Through the famine, the move to Egypt, and his final blessings, he cares for them all.

Jacob's journey is the journey of THREE. It takes the need to flee for his life to make him abandon his unhealthy competition with his brother. In the desert on the way to a foreign land, in that land for twenty years, and in the desert alone on the way back home, he is able to contemplate "the real Jacob," not the false self-image he likes to present. He finds "the real Jacob" – the one who meets with God in prayer – and in humbling himself before God, receives the promise of great blessings which can use his many gifts for good and not for ill. Jacob goes on to develop healthy non-competitive relationships, to promote and celebrate the gifts of others, and to learn for the future from all that has gone before.

Jacob's final duty – SIX – is to gather his sons for their final blessings (Genesis 49). It is a scene of serene peacefulness – a large and diverse family united: NINE. The text of that final blessing as we have it is all TWO and THREE and FOUR: the team leader – THREE – with strong and knowing "motherly" compassion – TWO – in the most beautiful poetic language – FOUR – bidding his final, ambiguous farewell.

NINE – Jonah

To find out what the prophets of Israel thought of Nineveh, we need look no further than the book of the prophet Nahum – an entire Old Testament book dedicated to its detailed condemnation. "Nineveh" would rank alongside "Babylon" as a name for all things utterly godless and wicked.

God asks Jonah to go there.

We only find out in Jonah 4:2 why Jonah does not want to go. He does not want Nineveh to be saved, and he knows that if he goes there, God will save it – being a gracious God, merciful, slow to anger, and abounding in love. To Jonah, the saving of Nineveh represents an unspeakable injustice against all that is right and good: his ONE wing could never allow it. Like Nahum, Jonah wants Nineveh destroyed: his EIGHT wing wants revenge against the unspeakable injustice of the continued existence of this powerful, successful, and evil place. God wants to save it and gut type Jonah wants no part in it.

For gut types, place is important, so Jonah took himself away. He did not struggle with his emotions, he did not argue with words, he just left the room – as NINE often will (Jonah 1:1-3).

And to communicate with gut types it is often best to use actions – rather than words or emotions. God uses a great storm. But Jonah, being NINE, is the only person on board the ship to sleep soundly through it all (Jonah 1:4-5).

With NINEs, what you see is what you get. They ask Jonah what is going on, and he explains quite plainly that he is a Hebrew, a servant of the great God who made the seas and the dry land, that he has fallen out with God and is running away from God, and that the storm is therefore certainly his fault (Jonah 1:6-12). That's NINE, just saying it plainly, saying it how it is.

The plain words of NINE can be incredibly effective. Those aboard ship are converted by Jonah's simple testimony. They give up crying to their own gods (Jonah 1:5) and call on the Lord instead (Jonah 1:14).

Jonah's plea that they resolve the crisis by throwing him into the sea (Jonah 1:12) is less selflessly generous than it might at first appear when we recognize what is going on for Jonah as NINE. Even here, in the midst of the storm, he does not want to engage his head or his emotions in the complexity of dealing with God's unreasonable request. Like the narcoticized NINE of today, he seeks a physical route to oblivion, to make it all go away: "keep it simple – just throw me into the sea and all this chaos will be over – yours and mine." The newly converted shipmates want to do no such thing to God's prophet, but soon appear to be left with no choice – and they throw him into the sea (Jonah 1:13-16).

Three days in the belly of the fish stop gut type Jonah from running away or making himself busy in order to avoid having to think or feel. As so often for the modern alcoholic, or any corrupted NINE, it is only when Jonah faces the real possibility of losing absolutely everything that he knows it is time to make a change (Jonah 2:4-5). It is time to connect with head and heart, and time to face the future and the past – time to face God (Jonah 2).

Round two (Jonah 3:1-2) and this time Jonah goes to Nineveh. He dutifully preaches (Jonah 3:4) – NINE's link to SIX. And he must have had about him something of the link to the inspiring leadership of THREE, because Nineveh repents (Jonah 3:5) and God answers their prayer that they might be saved from destruction (Jonah 3:6-10).

And at the end of it all, Jonah is displeased (Jonah 4:1). His ONE cannot bear the unfairness of forgiveness for such late repentance. His EIGHT still wants revenge for the years of evil. His slow-moving NINE cannot shift from the position it has maintained concerning Nineveh through his entire life. In his vengeful EIGHT and his judgmental ONE he is angry even at his own NINE vision of a gentle, peaceful, loving God (Jonah 4:2), and he longs once again to escape all this mental and emotional complexity and find oblivion (Jonah 4:3). He even leaves the city to sit on the hillside in the hope that he will see the fire come down to destroy the evil place (Jonah 4:5).

NINEs often feel contentedly invisible and like SIXes are charmed and surprised by attention, so Jonah is delighted when God grows him a plant for shade (Jonah 4:6) – but this is just part of another gutsy acted parable from God. When the plant dies, Jonah is angry about its destruction, and would have preferred that it had lived – and God says, forget the plant, you should feel this way about the city, delighted that it lives (Jonah 4:7-11).

Whether the book of Jonah is history or parable, it gives a truly remarkable portrait of NINE with all its gifts and all its failings. Jonah's NINE can be stubborn, complacent, neglectful, and fatalistic, and can go through idleness to the longing for oblivion. It can also be open and direct, steadfast and goal-oriented, able to speak hard truths calmly. Jonah's journey is the journey of NINE:

he had to find his gifts and his energy, his self-worth and his inner drive, reflect on his priorities, connect with head and heart, and then act.

ONE – Paul

Paul was a good Jewish boy: properly circumcised, having been born in Jewish blood in the tribe of Benjamin, he was determined to maintain this head start in his own choices, and he was the perfect pedantic Pharisee in the keeping of the law. He had every right to be proud, and he knew it (Philippians 3:4-5). This is all so very ONE.

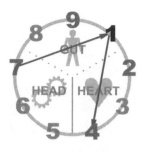

No doubt Paul observed every detail of the Old Testament food regulations (Matthew 15:11-12), tithed mint and dill and cumin (Matthew 23:23), criticized anyone who defiled the Sabbath by plucking grain or healing the sick (Luke 6:1-11), and never ate with sinners (Luke 15:2). The trouble is, this supposed level of perfection is humanly impossible to maintain. Those who seek to present themselves as perfect and righteous in the eyes of the law may or may not manage its minute practical details, but no human being ever achieves a perfection justifying self-righteousness in "the weightier matters of the law – justice and mercy and faith" (Matthew 23:23).

And this is the torment for ONEs. Their determination to be on their best behavior will serve them well in so many situations, but it is always on the brink of letting them down, when their inevitable imperfections show through and become a blot on the public image.

One attempt to resolve this is to try ever harder to achieve that perfect image – to tithe mint and dill and cumin, and in Paul's case, to persecute the followers of Jesus with more zeal than anybody else (Philippians 3:6). But the more ONE comes to rely on the perfect image, the more conscious ONE becomes of the imperfection within. Eventually, in some crisis moment, ONE will realize that the facade cannot be maintained any longer: as directly engaging gut types, ONEs cannot ultimately maintain any mask between their "inner self" and the outside world.

The moment of crisis comes for Paul on the road to Damascus – and by God's grace it becomes his moment of conversion (Acts 9:1-9). Paul is changed – but still ONE.

Paul now applies his methodical perfectionist ONE – with its limitless energy in the service of an ideal – to the task of proclaiming the good news he has found in Christ. The energy for all of this is coming from his gut: anger at the wasted years under "the law," anger at those who still promote the law – and inexpressible delight at the removal of that heavy burden, at having become "a new creation" (Galatians 6:15). Head logic and heart compassion are not always his most prominent gifts – but Paul is full of gutsy determination and energy in the service of his new ideal, and he has a kind of raw clarity in describing it.

Paul's gospel of ONE is this: that human perfection before God will never be found by human striving, but only through God's gracious work in the death and resurrection of Jesus Christ, received by the believer through faith. This thesis is set out in systematically ONEish style in the first four chapters of Paul's carefully honed letter to the Romans.

- God is indeed wrathful – ONE would be very much aware – not only at the lawlessness of the Gentiles (Romans 1:18-32) but also – Paul now realizes – at the hypocritical and judgmental proponents of the law at the other extreme (Romans 2).

- There are benefits in a good Jewish background, but they are not sufficient – notes ONE – for salvation (Romans 3:1-20).

- Having established our need, Paul presents God's answer to our need: the gift of God is righteousness for all believers, by grace, through faith – not through works or the law, lest any should boast – and for Jew and for Gentile alike (Romans 3:21-31).

- Living before the law was given, even Abraham was justified by faith and not by law (Romans 4).

The same argument makes up the whole of the earlier epistle to the Galatians, spelt out there with less of the tidy theology and far more passion, addressed as it is to one particular church in the wake of Paul's stand-up row with Peter in Antioch (Galatians 2).

Back in Romans, thriving now under the pressure of the task, Paul finds his FOUR, and writes four wonderfully poetic chapters celebrating the new life in Christ.

- We can rejoice in the assurance of salvation, which is reconciliation with God (Romans 5:1-11).

- We can rejoice that the new life means freedom: freedom from sin and death, with Christ as the victorious second Adam (Romans 5:12-21); freedom from sin and self through union with Christ (Romans 6); and freedom from the law (Romans 7) – "we are discharged from the law, which held us captive – we serve not under the old written code, but in the new life of the Spirit" (Romans 7:6).

- And we can rejoice that the Christian life is lived in the Spirit, is destined for glory, and makes us children of God (Romans 8).

Paul actually struggles to find the language to describe the new life in Christ. He knows that both utter lawlessness and total dependence on law are wrong, but he has no word for "good ethics" – in which he believes – apart from the word "law" – which he rejects – and so he struggles throughout his writing with the word and with the concept, as in Romans 7. In chapters 9 to 11 he struggles again with the relationship between God's promises to Israel and justification and salvation in Christ – forever seeking clarity – all so ONE.

Paul also struggles to find words to express the revolutionary change that comes about when this new means of salvation in Christ is received by the believer. To describe the contrast, and the ongoing struggle within the believer, he tries "old self" and "new self" or "old nature" and "new nature" (Ephesians 4:22-24;

Colossians 3:9-10), but slips most easily into using the Greek concepts "flesh" and "spirit" to mean "bad self" and "good self," "old way" and "new way." Many Greek philosophers really did believe that the flesh, the physical world, was bad, and the spirit, and all things non-physical, were good, but this dualism was not Paul's intention – indeed he would hardly have been able to grasp the concept. As a scholar of the Hebrew Scriptures, he would have been versed only in their view of the human being as fully integrated, body and soul – indeed the mark of God's covenant for Hebrew males is made "in the flesh." He saw salvation as won in the flesh and blood of Christ. He saw salvation as integration into the body of Christ. He promoted baptism and Eucharist and the laying-on of hands. And particularly as a gut type, nothing could be more artificial for Paul than the idea that body and spirit be considered separately, one saved and the other condemned. Paul simply adopts the words that the Greek philosophers use to mean "bad self" and "good self," and he uses them to mean no more and no less than that.

We have other examples of Paul finding his poetic FOUR in Philippians 2:1-11 – the song of Christ's glory – and in 1 Corinthians chapters 12 and 13 – the image of all Christians making up one body, and the hymn to love. The emphasis on union and love reveals the compassionate TWO wing. We see Paul's NINE wing in the prayer and the longing that people may have peace in their hearts and with one another (Romans 1:7; 12:18; 2 Corinthians 13:11 and elsewhere) – and ultimately know the peace of God which passes all understanding (Philippians 4:7). And Paul's SEVEN, once part of the driving force for excess zeal in persecution, is everywhere in the new Paul where he rejoices or tells us to rejoice, come what may (Acts 16:25; 1 Thessalonians 5:16; Philippians 4:4 – and Romans chapters 5 to 8 above).

Interestingly, in 1 Corinthians 2:1-5 Paul makes the point emphatically that he is not FIVE, which would be the diametric opposite of the ONE-and-NINE he there claims for himself: he has no lofty words of wisdom and his speech is imperfect, so he keeps the message simple – and the message is the embodied, gutsy

179

message of Jesus Christ crucified, backed up by a directly engaging "demonstration of the Spirit and power."

Paul remains ONE. The final justice of judgment at the return of Christ remains important to him – it is a major theme of both letters to the Thessalonians. Paul is endlessly arguing to justify himself – as in 1 Corinthians 9, and 1 Thessalonians 2, and at his most indignant in 2 Corinthians 10–13. He works out new laws and recommendations for the New Testament era (on marriage in 1 Corinthians 7, on the Roman government of the time in Romans 13:1-7) and he offers advice on awkward issues of conscience (as with food offered to idols in 1 Corinthians 8). He can bear a painful grudge like a true ONE (Acts 15:38), and he still likes his occasional slightly dissonant lists of who will be judged and condemned (1 Corinthians 6:9-10; Galatians 5:19-21). At least he balances them with methodically ONEish lists of the gifts of the redeemed (1 Corinthians 12:4-11; Galatians 5:22-23).

On a very personal and intimate note, Paul describes the struggle of ONE quite perfectly, quite beautifully, in 2 Corinthians 12:7 – that a "thorn in the flesh," an imperfection, a torment, prevents him from running away with any sense of his own perfection, any self-righteousness. To do that would be a sin, of course, so he gives thanks for the imperfection – he gives thanks for the very torment of being ONE.

God's message to Paul, and through Paul to all ONEs, is this: "My grace is sufficient for you, for my power is made perfect in weakness" – so Paul will now gladly boast of his weakness, that the power of Christ may rest upon him (2 Corinthians 12:9).

Paul's journey is the journey of ONE. He has to rebel against the internal critic – in his case "the law" – and how surely he does that. He stands up against it and asserts his freedom. And the perfection he has sought all his life he finds not in ever-greater effort – where it would never be found – but in the broken body and poured-out blood of the cross, the very symbol of failure and condemnation, but gloriously, miraculously transformed now, because God is there, God is in it, God is in the very brokenness of our broken humanity, in our life and in our death, and is now the pioneer of our resurrection.

TWO – John

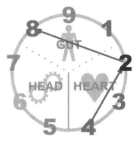

From the very beginning – from the lakeside in Galilee – John is part of that inner circle of disciples along with the brothers Peter and Andrew and his own brother James (Matthew 4:18-22). But John's relationship with Jesus could hardly be more different from Peter's. Peter is all head energy at SIX: faith and fear, loyalty and retreat, full of words – and nudging the boundaries of faith only by great feats of mental anguish. John is one of Peter's opposite types: TWO to Peter's SIX. In John's relationship with Jesus we see the compassion of the heart with the engagement of the gut: we see all of TWO.

There are hints of John's TWO in the gospel stories – but we see John's TWO supremely in his own writing.

Only a TWO could write such a movingly compassionate account of Jesus' encounter with the woman caught in adultery (John 8:1-11), or of Jesus' being so deeply moved at the death of Lazarus (John 11:33-36). Luke's Gospel contains a story where Jesus' feet are anointed with perfume and the ensuing argument is about the woman Jesus is allowing to do this (Luke 7:37-39): in John's Gospel, the person anointing is a known friend of the disciples, and the argument is about whether such extravagant luxury is justified in a world of need. For John, for Jesus, it is justified: this is the intimacy and compassion of TWO.

John's TWO is seen most clearly in his account of the Last Supper. John omits entirely any account of the breaking of the bread or the sharing of the cup, which are gifts from Jesus to the disciples as a group and to the world. Instead, John alone relates another event from that evening, an event which will have meant far more to John as TWO – not a gift from Jesus to the world or to the group, but a gift to each one of them, one at a time: the washing of their feet. One by one, Jesus will have touched them, held them, looked into their eyes, and then performed this act of service: physical, and all from the heart; pure TWO, and imprinted in every vivid detail on John's memory (John 13:1-11).

John sets the context at the very beginning of this account: Jesus has "loved his own in the world, and loved them to the end," and prepares now to "depart out of this world to the Father"; Jesus "knows that the Father has given all things into his hands, and that he comes from God and is going to God." This is all about love and relationship (John 13:1-3).

John then gives the account of the foot-washing, and after it, Jesus' immediate explanation: it is all about serving one another, one to one, within the fellowship of disciples, in accordance with the example that he has given (John 13:12-15) – and to serve one another within the fellowship of the disciples is to serve Jesus himself (John 13:20).

Jesus' new commandment is that the disciples are to love one another as Jesus himself has loved them: indeed this is how those outside the fellowship of the disciples will recognize those who are within (John 13:34-35; 15:12,17). Relationship with God now means a one-to-one love-relationship with Jesus (John 14:6-11,18-24; 15:13-16) who incorporates the disciples into himself, the living vine, by love (John 15:1-10), and who sends a comforter to continue his work among them (John 14:15-17,25-26; 16:7-15).

Despite all that lies ahead for Jesus himself, John does not present Jesus as we see him in the other Gospels – tormented in the garden of Gethsemane – but calm and collected, caring only about how the disciples must be feeling: "Let not your hearts be troubled – I go to prepare a place for you – I will come back for you – peace be with you" (John 14:1-3,27; 16:16-33). This is an account of the evening as remembered by TWO.

It is John who "lies close to the breast of Jesus" at the supper itself (John 13:23).

At the cross, wherever the others may have been (Luke 23:49), John is standing right there with the three women: Jesus' mother, and her sister, and Mary Magdalene. Jesus commends his mother and John to each other, to care for one another as mother and son. It is a perfect TWO moment (John 19:25-27).

And throughout the telling of this story, John refers to himself as "the disciple whom Jesus loved" – a self-identification, however accidental, of John's self-image as TWO.

We have just three other glimpses of John in the other Gospels – all of them very TWO, none of them very flattering. In a particularly TWOish lapse, it is James and John together who seek special places in the coming kingdom, right by Jesus' side: Jesus very gently smoothes things over when this causes the inevitable indignation among the others, using the event as an opportunity to teach about service (Mark 10:35-45; Matthew 20:20-28 – in Matthew's account their mother appears to talk them into it). Fiercely protective of Jesus, it is John who complains that they have seen someone who is not among their number using Jesus' name to cast out demons; John tries to forbid him, because for TWO, relationship is what matters, and this person is not in relationship; Jesus says to leave well alone (Mark 9:38, Luke 9:49). Soon after this, again fiercely TWOishly protective of Jesus, James and John ask whether fire should be called down from heaven to consume the villages which have rejected Jesus, just because he is heading for Jerusalem; Jesus again calls them to back off (Luke 9:51-56). This confrontational flash of anger in the service of TWO must be either the ONE wing of TWO or TWO's link to EIGHT. Either way, it helps to explain how Jesus comes to surname gentle TWOish John and his brother James "the sons of thunder" (Mark 3:17) – the thunder heard when heart type TWO finds their anger in the ONE wing or in confrontational stress type EIGHT.

Just as Peter thrives after the resurrection, so it is with John. At some point they had become a key partnership: Jesus sent them together to prepare the Last Supper (Luke 22:8), and in John's account of resurrection morning, they run together to the empty tomb after Mary Magdalene arrives with the news. Heart type

John stands respectfully outside, stooping to look in, and wondering; head type Peter goes straight in to see what there is to see (John 20:1-7). Subsequently Peter and John are together through the early chapters of Acts: in the temple together in chapter 3, arrested together in chapter 4, and traveling to Samaria to minister together in Acts 8:14-25. Head type Peter does most of the public speaking, but John is right there by his side. For as long as they were able to work together, Peter and John will have made a compelling partnership – complementing each other superbly as opposite types, SIX and TWO, bringing a whole range of gifts and touching a whole range of people. Although they worked separately rather than together, Peter and Paul also make a formidable "partnership" for the spread of the gospel, as opposite types SIX and ONE, ensuring that a whole range of gifts is brought to the task of reaching a whole range of people. John may have been influential in securing the converted Paul's endorsement by Peter and James (Galatians 2:9); Paul and John are very different characters, but Paul, ONE, does have his TWO wing, and John, TWO, does have his ONE wing, so they would have been able to relate to each other. The complementary influences of these three – Peter, Paul, and John – bring many gifts to the service of the gospel – in the first century and in every century since.

The three New Testament letters attributed to John continue the TWO theme. The key theme in discussing forgiveness is not a great cosmic plan, as described by Paul, but relationship: we confess to God, and God forgives (1 John 1:9); Jesus pleads for us as our advocate (1 John 2:1); and now God loves us with an overwhelming love, calling us children of God (1 John 3:1). You must love (1 John 2:10; 1 John 3:11; 1 John 4:7), and it matters what you love – it must be God and one another, not the things of the world (1 John 2:15-17) – and it matters how you love – it must be seen in practical TWOish acts of service for those in need, not just in pious words (1 John 3:17-18). In 1 John 4, the perfect statement of the TWO gospel appears twice: that God is love (1 John 4:8,16). From this develops a full, ONEish systematic theology of salvation based on love (1 John 4:7-21). The second letter repeats the themes; the third again promotes "rendering service to the brethren" (3 John 1:5).

In John we have seen the angry wing ONE, and now the systematic wing ONE. In John's shared leadership of the early Church we see the emergence of the leading and inspiring wing THREE. TWO's link to creative FOUR is seen in John's writing – his Greek text is poetic and elegant throughout, and the classic translations capture this superbly in the well-known prologue to the Gospel ("In the beginning was the Word..." – John 1:1-18). We see TWO's link to EIGHT in the letters: John explicitly instructs us to "test people out" in 1 John 4:1-6, and throughout the epistles he keeps on EIGHTishly asserting, very strongly, that love which fails to produce practical action is no love at all (1 John 2:9,11; 1 John 3:14-15; 1 John 4:8 – and also the assertiveness of 1 John 1:6,8,10). But above all John is TWO. From Galilee to the writings, for John, "God is love."

John's journey is part of the journey of TWO. When he asked for the seat at Jesus' right hand in the kingdom, he thought it could be all about Jesus and him: that was all that mattered to him. When he wanted to call down fire on the villages that rejected Jesus, or forbid the freelance healer who used Jesus' name, again nothing mattered but immediate close intimacy with Jesus – and Jesus corrected him both times. John had to widen his vision and realize that God's plans were bigger than just himself and his immediate friends: God has a much wider plan for the good of the whole world.

The writings of John are all about love. He manages to move beyond the TWOish idea that it is only about Jesus and John – but characteristically in John's writing, the command to love is for Christians to love Christians: John manages to extend his vision from the one-to-one love relationship to love within a community, but not quite to the point of anonymous "good Samaritan" love, beyond the known community (Luke 10:29-37), or the radical call to love your enemies (Matthew 5:44; Luke 6:27,35). John's particular contribution to the work of God's love in the world is the compassionate, generous, caring, individually focused love of TWO.

FOUR – Isaiah

Isaiah's great call and commissioning took place "in the year that King Uzziah died". Uzziah had ruled Judah for fifty-two years, so this was a year of great change and instability for the nation – already a dramatic moment for Isaiah and for Judah. True to his call and commissioning, Isaiah becomes prophet to a whole generation – active through four reigns and four decades.

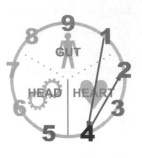

The setting for the call is the temple in Jerusalem, and its form is a dramatic and glorious vision. The Lord is seated on a throne, "high and exalted," and his glory fills the temple. Six-winged seraphs are in attendance, calling "holy, holy". The whole building shakes and fills with smoke. It could be the incense of heaven or it could be the dust of the earthquake: either way it is dramatic and unsettling (Isaiah 6:1-4).

In the midst of all this drama, Isaiah faces God in awe and bewails his unworthiness and his inevitable demise. God offers a purifying forgiveness: a seraph brings a coal from the altar, touches Isaiah's lips, and says, "your guilt has departed and your sin is blotted out" (Isaiah 6:5-7).

The situation is transformed in that moment. Now when God says "Whom shall I send?" Isaiah can reply: "Here am I, send me" (Isaiah 6:8).

This is all very FOUR: to experience such glories in visions and dreams; to record them in striking poetry; and the very business of being commissioned by God as an individual – a unique individual with a message for the world.

Isaiah's initial sense of unworthiness is FOUR clinging to security type ONE. God addresses this link to ONE with the assurance of purification and forgiveness – so when the challenge comes – "Whom shall I send?" – Isaiah can thrive under pressure and move to volunteering TWO: "send me."

Finally Isaiah is challenged to stay true to the task – even when the people neither see nor understand (Isaiah 6:9-10), and even through all the pain that lies ahead (Isaiah 6:11-13): a call to the true vocation of FOUR.

The five chapters leading up to this account are a summary of Isaiah's message. It begins with observations and descriptions – as the state of the nation is assessed by observer FIVE on the wing of FOUR. God and the nation are "utterly estranged" as the country "lies desolate" (Isaiah 1:2-8) – and yet the practice of their religion continues regardless (Isaiah 1:11).

Isaiah describes God as disgusted at this dissonance between outer religion and inner iniquity (Isaiah 1:11-15). Disgust is a gut reaction – caused here by the "imperfection" of godlessness – FOUR's link again to gut type ONE. God is appalled at their very presence, "this trampling of my courts": location and presence are important in the gut zone (Isaiah 1:12). And on the wing of ONE at NINE, Isaiah has God going all passive-aggressive: averting his eyes and covering his ears as they approach with their unworthy prayers (Isaiah 1:15). "Wash yourselves, make yourselves clean" says the text – meaning: "learn to do good, seek justice, correct oppression, defend the orphan, plead for the widow" (Isaiah 1:16-17). This is idealism, addressing impurity – this is ONE.

And now Isaiah's God woos us, and offers to make things right: FOUR's link to TWO. "Come now, let us reason together, says the Lord; though your sins are like scarlet, they shall be as white as snow" (Isaiah 1:18). And typically for TWO, this section is both wooing and demanding: only if you are "willing and obedient" will you eat the good of the land; refusal and rebellion lead inevitably to destruction by the sword (Isaiah 1:19-20).

Chapter 2 begins with a beautiful vision of a perfect world. All the nations flow to the house of the Lord, on the highest of all mountains. God will be judge, and in this idealistic utopia, swords will be beaten into ploughshares, and spears into pruning hooks, and nations will speak of peace and not war. The poetry and imagery of FOUR express the idealistic and peaceful visions of the link to ONE – and its NINE wing (Isaiah 2:1-4).

Chapter 5 declares itself to be a love song – bringing together the poetry of FOUR and the intimate compassion of TWO. It is sung for a lover who has received all due attention, but like a failing vineyard yielded no good fruit: it is a TWOish lament for an asymmetry of love where for all of the giving there has been no fair response (Isaiah 5:1-7).

Many years later, "second Isaiah" writes the moving description of the suffering servant of God – bringing so much to our New Testament understanding of Jesus as Messiah and Redeemer. The righteous suffering servant of God grows up among us, "does no violence," and "has no deceit in his mouth" – but is rejected and cast out, persecuted and despised. Somehow through his suffering redemption comes – and a salvation that spreads beyond Israel to the world (Isaiah 52:13–53:12). This is truly the vision and vocation of FOUR: bringing redemption – often for others – through the pain.

In Isaiah we see the poetry and the pain and the creativity and the empathy of FOUR – and the anger and justice and idealism of the link to ONE, and the demanding compassion of the link to TWO. We see the objective observation of the FIVE wing, and the gifts of wing THREE as the writer inspires hope for a future redeemer. Adding in the vision of peace at NINE, Isaiah uses the gifts of every sector that FOUR can reach – continuous from sector NINE to sector FIVE.

In the section on "access all areas," we noted that FOUR has no easy access to sectors SIX or SEVEN or EIGHT. Isaiah's only interest in the following of detailed rules is to condemn it as an inadequate disgrace: there is no easy comfort here for a particular kind of SIX. Where Isaiah has messages of joy, they are visions for the future – not SEVEN's call to be positive in the literal here and now. And Isaiah's attacks on the powerful are poetry based on observation – not action based on instinct: Isaiah is an observing poet, not an instinctive fighter EIGHT.

Isaiah's journey is the journey of FOUR: from praying alone in the temple, seeing profound visions, and thinking deep thoughts – to engaging with the people, communicating profoundly and with great beauty, and serving and challenging as a prophet of God.

Of course many hands have contributed to the book of Isaiah as we receive it today. Its consistency comes from its faithfulness to a single ideal and style – and it is not only "the several Isaiahs," but the prophets as a group, who are corporately FOUR – or at least in the heart zone. When Jesus speaks of the Old Testament, he speaks of "the law and the prophets." Those from Moses onward who gave Israel its laws were working from the head side to influence the behavior of the people: the prophets were working from the heart side, to the same end. Each from their own perspective, the law and the prophets seek to exert a godly influence on the choices and behavior of the people – one from the head, and one from the heart.

FIVE – Psalm 73

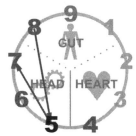

The Old Testament begins with seventeen books of history and concludes with the seventeen books of the prophets. In between come the five books of wisdom or poetry: Job, Psalms, Proverbs, Ecclesiastes, and the Song of Songs.

The book of Psalms is a collection of songs and poems from many different writers. One hundred of the psalms have titles naming an author: seventy-three name David; eleven name "the sons of Korah"; two name Solomon; Moses and Ethan are named once each – and Asaph is named for Psalm 73 and eleven others.

Psalm 73 is classic work of observing, deep-thinking FIVE.

In the early verses, the psalmist observes the world as if from afar – and does not like what he sees: he is distressed at the prosperity of the wicked (Psalm 73:2-3).

It was a commonplace at that time, throughout the interacting cultures of the region, to believe that the righteous would prosper and the wicked would come to nothing – that the good would be rewarded and the evil would be punished. Psalm 1 and Psalm 37 both proclaim this theme. This is the cause of distress for our observer FIVE in Psalm 73: Asaph observes that the wicked are prosperous, and this is sufficient challenge to his faith that his "feet are close to stumbling" (Psalm 73:2). The full scale of the injustice he sees is described in verses 4 to 9: the wicked and arrogant are also proud and violent, and full of spite and folly – and yet they are healthy, well fed, untroubled, and powerful. This is the objective analysis of the observer FIVE.

It gets worse: people are turning to these evildoers and proclaiming on account of their prosperity that God clearly pays no regard to good and evil. People who live regular, difficult lives – "stricken all day long, chastened every morning" – are deciding that their efforts to live righteously have been wasted efforts, because in contrast to their own ordinary, difficult lives, it seems that "the wicked are always at ease, and increase in riches" (Psalm 73:10-14).

Asaph paints these observations in vivid colors – the FOUR wing of FIVE – and there is a clear temptation to envy – also on the FOUR wing of FIVE. And now we see the faithful, loyal SIX wing of FIVE deeply distressed as all that it knows of God is challenged (Psalm 73:16): Asaph is tempted even to go along with those who are turning to the wicked, but that would be untrue to all that he has held dear – untrue to all that he knows (Psalm 73:15). Therefore, he sticks with what he knows: he goes faithfully to the sanctuary despite everything – and it is there, in prayer before God, that all becomes clear to him once again (Psalm 73:17). There he recounts what he knows: that the downfall of the wicked will be great in the end; that the place of wickedness is a dangerous place, whatever prosperity may be there; that while there may be prosperity in wickedness for a while, there is no security, and nothing of eternal value to be found (Psalm 73:17-20,27).

It is a painful and difficult thing for SIX to move a boundary, to change an understanding. Based on his FIVE observations,

Asaph's SIX wing has nudged the definition of the lot of the wicked from "nothing good in this world" to "nothing good that lasts". It was a move sufficiently important to justify his FOUR wing's creating a Psalm.

Asaph repents of his earlier doubting, and gives thanks for God's faithfulness throughout – and for God's faithfulness into eternity (Psalm 73:21-24). God is his sober joy, his one desire, strong and sufficient forever, despite the envy and despite the pain: this is Asaph touching a redeemed SEVEN – which is FIVE thriving under pressure (Psalm 73:25-26,28). And the security type EIGHT is also here – as Asaph foresees the final downfall of the prosperous wicked (Psalm 73:18-20,27).

In the earlier section on "access all areas," we noted that FIVE has no easy access to ONE or TWO or THREE. In the early verses of the psalm Asaph observes the injustice of the world but he feels only sadness and bewilderment – not the inflamed anger at unfairness which is so distinctive to ONE. On finding his own resolution in the temple he is not suddenly overcome with compassion for the wicked as individuals or determined to go out and woo them back to God one by one – which would have been the instinct of TWO. Neither does he feel the burden to win them back to God as a group – which would have been the vocation of THREE. For Asaph the observer, it is enough to tell faithfully of God's works and God's goodness to any who will hear, while the wicked go the way that they will go (Psalm 73:27-28). Asaph has wisdom for those who choose to seek it, and will tell of it as he can – and this is the vocation of FIVE.

Asaph's journey was the journey of FIVE. He needed to make a decision about how he would live. He reached a point where he had to interpret what he knew and apply it to his life, even though it was difficult to understand. To do this he went to the temple, where in quietness he could still, or rise above, the endlessly churning mind – and there he learned to see the wisdom of ordinary humble goodness, compared to the vain glory of the prosperous: he learned that true wisdom is a simple, righteous life.

The five Old Testament books of "wisdom" are well named – for they all show aspects of FIVE throughout. Distinctively within the Old Testament, they incorporate philosophical ideas that derive from the creative interaction of many cultures – although they come to us through faithfully Hebrew selection and discernment.

During the reigns of David and Solomon, Israel was a proud and wealthy nation, attracting visitors from far and wide. Centuries earlier, Abraham, Isaac, and Jacob had traveled often and traveled widely – from Ur near the Persian Gulf in the east to Egypt in the west. Later, during the time of the exile a single empire covered territories "from India to Ethiopia" (Esther 1:1) – and influences from even that far afield can be detected in the books of wisdom.

The ideal of wisdom was highly prized in all those eastern cultures: to observe and understand the details of how the world worked, to distil the wisdom from the observation, and then to teach it and pass it on, in public or in private.

The book of Proverbs comes directly from this tradition. It is a book of head wisdom: pieces of advice, each in a short, punchy, memorable format – in words – based on observations of the world around, observations of how the world works. It attempts no great theology or understanding of any great divine plan. It just says: this is how it is, and this is how to deal with it.

A universal concept for faith across all the cultures of the region was the conviction that everybody, good or bad, must surely get what they deserve in the end – the eastern religions call it karma. This is not a Hebrew concept – from the history of the Hebrew people – and yet it is found in many of the Psalms, and the Hebrew scholars have to address it, as we have seen in our review of Psalm 73. The problem is that it does not appear to be universally true: people do not always get what they deserve in the end; often they get better or worse than they "deserve." As well as being the subject of Psalm 73, this is the subject of two whole books from the wisdom section – Job and Ecclesiastes.

Ecclesiastes, observing the state of things at FIVE, produces beautiful poetry at the FOUR wing – and great sadness at the SIX wing, because there does not seem to be any simple rule to make everything all right. The writer's solution is to be content with what there is: to stay happy – the link to SEVEN – come what may. This almost has hints of the kind of eastern philosophy that became Buddhism – to choose to disconnect from suffering and to be content – though the idea is filtered through Hebrew scholars to be true Hebrew Scripture.

The book of Job is more complex, with Job's comforters insisting – in accordance with convention – that his suffering must be the result of sin (Job 4–31) – until Elihu brings God into it, suggesting that the wisdom of God could be far more complex, and way beyond our understanding, and that we should not dare to question it. This Job concedes, and then God speaks to confirm it (Job 32–37). God who is wise beyond our understanding may send things to try us, or discipline us like a loving parent – or just see and understand things that are beyond the reach of our human minds. This is one carefully thought out solution to the problem of suffering – a scholarly work of FIVE.

The most wonderful thing about the Song of Songs is that it was included at all in the collection of books that we acknowledge as Scripture. Its two lovers sing their passion and celebrate each other's sensual physicality. In the poetry of FOUR it is a FIVE observation that sex and sensuality are wonderful things. If the book had been left out of the Bible, there would have been no explicit celebration of the joy of physical sexuality in our Scriptures – but they put it in, so there is – our own gentle karma sutra.

And finally the book of Psalms itself contains fragments of ideas from many sources – such as repeated references to "the gods" (Psalm 82:1; Psalm 82:6; Psalm 86:8; Psalm 97:7) – as well as distinctively Hebrew texts – like an entire history of the nation in Psalm 78. And all of it is edited and compiled – by wise and studious FIVEs – for the people of the one true God of Israel – as their book, their collected poetry and wisdom, their Scripture.

SEVEN – Solomon

When Solomon is king of Israel, his daily provisions are 20 tons of flour, ten fat oxen, twenty pastured cattle, and a hundred sheep – besides harts, gazelles, roebucks, and fowl (1 Kings 4:22-23).

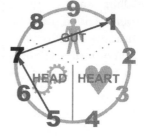

To build the temple he uses 30,000 forced laborers to collect wood from Lebanon, plus 80,000 quarrymen, 70,000 general laborers, and 3,300 supervisors. It takes seven years (1 Kings 5:13-16).

Everything is made of gold or covered in gold: Solomon imports twenty tons of gold per year. Even his household cups are made of gold. "Nothing was made of silver, because it was not considered as anything in the days of Solomon" (1 Kings 6:21; 10:14,21).

While building the temple, Solomon builds six other palaces and public buildings "of like workmanship" (1 Kings 7:1-8).

Solomon has seven hundred wives and three hundred concubines (1 Kings 11:3).

Perhaps all of this is gluttony and excess. Perhaps it is a righteously exuberant celebration of the goodness of God. Either way, it is most certainly SEVEN.

Even before the end of the reign of King David, Solomon and his brother Adonijah are rivals for the throne. When David makes clear his preference for Solomon, the issue is effectively settled: Adonijah's court disbands and Solomon makes peace with him (1 Kings 1:1-53). It all goes wrong when Adonijah approaches Solomon with a request – for the hand of a member of Solomon's household in marriage. Adonijah comes humbly and in peace, and even approaches Solomon through an intermediary, but still Solomon's anger flares up, and he has Adonijah executed at once – without further discussion, and without even meeting him. Two of Adonijah's former supporters are also executed and another is exiled (1 Kings 2:1-46). It may even have been a misunderstanding – but Solomon probably feared at that moment for the security of his kingdom. Under pressure, he went to his stress type, the angry ONE, who is also the ONE who likes to see a job completed and perfected with all the loose ends tied up – hence the executions and the exile. In a blaze of anger, Solomon destroys the former rivals with whom he has so recently made peace.

Now God intervenes to determine what this new king Solomon will become. In a dream, God appears to Solomon and invites Solomon to ask one thing of God. Solomon's reply is humble, very much aware of the awesome responsibility he holds, and of the model set by his father David – to which he refers. He is at his SIX wing, clinging to what he knows, and seeking to be loyal to his father's memory and to God. And now in this key moment, before the awesome presence of God, Solomon goes to his security type FIVE, and asks for this: that he might have an understanding mind to govern God's people; that he might be able to discern between good and evil. He asks for wisdom. This pleases God, and God grants his request, and so the legendary wisdom of Solomon is found (1 Kings 3:3-14). It could well be that Solomon now spends the rest of his reign feeling confident and secure – and living life on the SEVEN-FIVE axis.

The first test of Solomon's wisdom is when two harlots come to him in a dispute about a child: both had given birth; one child had died; each claimed that the living child was their own. Solomon tests them out – his EIGHT wing – in a most uncompromising manner, suggesting the child be divided in two, using a sword, that they might have half each. This is the EIGHT wing pushing at the very limits, as EIGHTs will. The real mother pleads for the life of the child, giving up any claim on her half in order that it might live: the pretender would have been happy to see it die – and Solomon awards the child to its mother (1 Kings 3:15-28).

The wisdom of Solomon is assumed to form the basis of the book of Proverbs. In its opening chapters, the book of Proverbs stresses the importance of teaching wisdom from one generation to the next. It then provides countless one-line pieces of written advice. As detailed, written advice, to be taught down the generations, the advice of the book of Proverbs is not to "go with your gut instincts" or "go with your heart": rather it is head zone advice, and therefore very SIX – "stick with what you know." This is Solomon on the SIX wing of both home base SEVEN and security and wisdom link FIVE.

Toward the end of his life, Solomon's heart was led astray by his SEVENish excess: his many wives turned his heart to many gods (1 Kings 11:1-13). This is blamed for the division of the kingdom into two immediately following Solomon's death – but it is also interesting to note which single sector of the board is inaccessible to SEVEN. SEVEN has no easy access to the leadership and team-building of THREE. Solomon may have built a fine temple and led the nation into times of great prosperity, but he did not have the gifts of THREE to hold the nation together.

If the attribution of the book of Ecclesiastes to Solomon is correct, then in his old age Solomon reflected on all that had gone before. Deep into FIVEish observation of all that had been, he notes the material excesses of his life, and reflects that the simple pleasures are the most important. He reflects in often poetic, FOURish verse – and his final advice is not to think about it all too deeply after all, but to stick with what you know, and stay happy come what may. In his reflection, Solomon's journey is the journey of SEVEN: finally facing the pain of the world – its potential "vanity" or "emptiness" – he has slowed down, resolved to see the beauty and the joy in simple things, and learned that God has a place and a time for everything, not just the radiant.

EIGHT – Miriam, Deborah, and Hannah

Because of the culture and the times from which they emerge, it is not easy to make it into the narratives of the Bible as a woman. Only a particular kind of story makes it into Scripture: women are mostly either written out of the story, or excluded from the action in the first place. Strong women EIGHTs are the women most likely to make it  through into the text – and here are three of them: Miriam, Deborah, and Hannah.

We only glimpse Miriam in Exodus 15 and Numbers 12, but the hints that we do see suggest that she was alongside her two brothers, the leaders Moses and Aaron, throughout the escape from Egypt and in the years that followed. We read her EIGHTish character in Exodus 15, where she leads the people in singing a great celebration of their escape from Egypt. More than anything else, this focuses on issues of power: the way in which their powerful God has humiliated and utterly destroyed their enemy. Nowhere in eighteen verses does it pause to consider the sadness of the fate of the Egyptian soldiers or their families: in this song, a mighty and righteous power has triumphed gloriously over evil, and will do so again and again. This attitude "keeps it simple" – which is the NINE wing; rejoicing in every detail of the sheer excess of the triumph reveals the SEVEN wing. The detailed account of what has happened, and its analysis as a work of God, reveals the link to observer FIVE. If there is a link to TWO here, it is to see God as the loving parent of the nation in verse 13 (Exodus 15:1-18,20-21).

The EIGHTish song of Deborah in Judges 5 is also a song of Israel's triumph, concluding triumphantly: "so perish all thine enemies, O Lord!" Deborah was one of several informally emerging leaders of Israel known as judges in the period between the entry into the promised land – led by Joshua at Jericho – and the anointing of the first king, Saul. Once again in this EIGHTish song of triumph we see EIGHT's link to observer FIVE in detailed descriptions of recent events – but here we also see a much stronger link to TWO. Deborah lists and occasionally chides the role of each tribe in turn in the recent campaign – and she is proclaimed "mother of the nation" (Judges 4 and 5).

Finally, Hannah gives us the prayer which Mary the mother of Jesus adapts to become the Magnificat in Luke chapter 2 – as used in the daily prayers of the church. Hannah's prayer celebrates the birth of her firstborn Samuel: Mary's prayer responds to the blessing spoken first by the angel and then, in the weeks following, by her cousin Elizabeth. Both prayers proclaim that God alone is the all-powerful one, raising up the lowly and casting down the mighty at will. This God shows mercy to those who stand in awe of him, and guards his faithful ones – but strikes down the mighty, and scatters the proud and their vanities. Those who were once rich and powerful will now go laboring to survive – or "be sent empty away" – while the hungry will be hungry no more, but "filled with good things."

In this prayer of EIGHT, Hannah has a beautiful link to the compassionate love of TWO in some lines of worship and adoration: "There is none holy as the Lord; there is none beside thee." God is then named as a "rock": EIGHT says "test this out – this is solid." This is the solid rock of a God who keeps the promises made many generations ago. And there is also a link to the observing FIVE: God is a God of knowledge, watching and weighing our actions.

We see the NINE wing of EIGHT in the celebration of simple faithfulness, simple humility, and simplicity of life: "keeping it simple." And we see the SEVEN wing of EIGHT in the rejoicing: "my heart exults," "my spirit rejoices in God" (1 Samuel 2:1-10; Luke 1:46-55).

We see too little of Miriam, Deborah, and Hannah to plot their journeys – but the usual journey of EIGHT sees power-conscious EIGHTs learning to respect others, finding the ability to show mercy, discovering the protector instinct, and finding the gentle heart within. All three of these women are heroes of the Scriptures, but perhaps Deborah was one step further on the road than Miriam – albeit in easier times – and perhaps Hannah was one step beyond Deborah, with her concern for the raising up of the lowly.

It is Hannah's prayer, through Mary, which becomes a daily prayer for the church – and EIGHT's contribution to our daily prayer. "My soul proclaims the greatness of the Lord: my spirit rejoices in God my savior; for he has looked with favor on his lowly servant. He has filled the hungry with good things, and the rich he has sent away empty: he has remembered his promise of mercy, made to our forebears, for Abraham and his children for ever."

Jesus – the perfect whole

"There are diverse gifts, but the same Spirit, and diverse ministries, but the same Lord, and diverse works, but the same God working all of them in every one. For just as the body has many parts, and all the parts make one body, so it is with Christ" (1 Corinthians 12:4-6,12).

Paul goes on to emphasize the way in which this diversity is essential to the functioning of the body. No part is any more or less important than any other. Every member has its part to play.

"So it is with Christ": it takes all of us to make up the body of Christ today, and none is any more or any less important than any other. The gifts of every type are essential to the life and work of the body of Christ on earth. Our diversity is vital, and so is our unity.

And just as the body of Christ today contains the whole variety of humankind, so also Jesus in the years of his earthly ministry embodied the whole variety of humankind. All nine strategies – all nine types – are found together, uniquely balanced and uniquely perfected, in Jesus of Nazareth.

Let us begin at EIGHT, with the Jesus many people least like to see, the Jesus they least like to quote: the Jesus who is energized, confrontational, and challenging. But we need this Jesus: the Jesus who recognizes where power lies, and fights for the powerless.

In Mark 3:1-6, Jesus heals on the Sabbath – which is forbidden – right there in the synagogue, quite knowingly and deliberately in full sight of the disapproving religious authorities. There is nothing discrete about this healing. This is no hidden rule-breaking, where nobody will know. This is a deliberate challenge, right in the face of his enemies. Jesus does what he does, right there in front of them, and they do indeed go out immediately to plot against him. This is Jesus kicking the boundaries and breaking the rules and aggressively challenging the powerful – for the sake of the weak. This is Jesus at EIGHT.

There is an EIGHT proclamation in Jesus' teaching, which we too often avoid. We like to hear Jesus calling the humble and the lowly to come up higher, and we love to proclaim that message – but Jesus also took time to condemn the haughty and the hypocritical. Jesus made an analysis of the power structures around him and daringly shouted down those who abused them. There is a whole chapter of this in Matthew 23: "woe to you, blind guides, hypocrites, whitewashed tombs, murderers – the blood of the prophets is upon you." There are thirty-six verses of this. Only for the final three verses of the chapter does EIGHT go to TWO, as it often will, and Jesus longs to mother Jerusalem like a mother-hen gathering her brood under her wings. These three verses are quoted far more often than the other thirty-six, but Jesus can be confrontational EIGHT just as much as wooing TWO.

The cleansing of the temple in John 2:13-15 sounds like angry aggressive EIGHT, kicking hard against the boundaries of what is possible – or ONE, with a blaze of anger at the impurity being wrought upon the place – but there is one small phrase, only here in John's account, which reveals the event to be far more carefully planned than any burst of anger. In verse 14, Jesus finds the temple full of traders – but before the driving out in the second half of verse 15, in the first half of the verse he makes a lash out of ropes. This must have taken some considerable time – so the event is far more carefully considered than we sometimes imagine. Jesus goes to see the temple. He leaves. He decides what to do. And then he does it. He makes a lash of ropes: a slow piece of handicraft – there is plenty of time here to ponder what is about to happen. And then he returns to the temple and drives his way through it – like an elephant about its task. This is not a burst of anger. This is NINE finding its calmly focused energy, and following through a plan, unstoppable once begun.

There is something very NINE about the parable of the sower (Luke 8:9-15). We often take this as a model for the outreach work of the church, and worry about the success or otherwise of our efforts – whether they bear fruit in the proper abundance. The wonderful reassurance of this parable is that the sower is never criticized. The sower's only task is to throw that seed – to get it out into the environment. The sower is not criticized for the fact that some falls on the rock and some falls in the shrubbery and some is carried away by the birds. The sower is just to keep on sowing regardless, and not to fret – for some will fall on good soil, and yield a hundredfold.

And the beautiful call of Jesus at NINE is this: "Come to me, all you who labor and are heavily burdened, and I will give you rest" (Matthew 11:28-30). Into the wearying complexity of our lives comes this simple call to come to Jesus, there to find our rest and our perfect peace.

Elsewhere Jesus sleeps peacefully in the stern of the boat while a storm rages around – and then he calms the storm: this is also Jesus at NINE (Mark 4:35-41).

The Sermon on the Mount is Jesus at ONE – the idealist and the perfectionist. Time and again in Matthew 5 Jesus quotes the Old Testament law – "you have heard it said" – and then he takes it further, takes it back to its ideals and toward the perfect: "you have heard it said ... but I say to you." You have heard it said that murder is wrong, but I say to you that anger and insult are sinful as well. You have heard it said that adultery is wrong, but I say to you that to look with lust is a sin. You have heard it said that you must perform the oath you swear, but I say to you that you should fulfill what you say without the need for any oath. You have heard it said that your retaliation should be limited and proportionate – an eye for an eye and a tooth for a tooth – but I say to you, do not retaliate at all. You have heard it said that you should love your friends and hate your enemies, but I say to you that you should love your enemies as well. The entire sermon – there are two more chapters – is a celebration of the idealism and perfectionism of ONE, of the orderly complete comprehensive teaching skills of ONE – and of ONE's link to FOUR, where clarity becomes poetry.

Whenever Jesus acts from compassion Jesus is at TWO – and the most supreme moment is the washing of the disciples' feet in John 13:3-9. In the chapters that follow, Jesus talks repeatedly about the love that flows between the Father, and himself, and the disciples. To the earlier commandments – love God, love your neighbor, and even love your enemies (Matthew 5:43-48; 22:34-40) – he adds the more intimate "love one another as I have loved you" (John 15:12). All of this is TWO. In the most practical TWO commandment, Jesus explicitly states that the one who wishes to be great should aim for the role of servant, and the one who wishes to be first should be like a slave, "even as the Son of man came not to be served but to serve" (Matthew 20:25-28).

The way in which Jesus deals gently with his small band of disciples shows Jesus very clearly at THREE, leading and inspiring and building up the team. After his baptism and the temptations in the wilderness, Jesus begins as an inspiring leader working alone – which THREE can be (Luke 4:14-21) – but not long afterwards, he is able to commission a team of no fewer than seventy to continue in the same work. He remains very much alongside them, inspiring and enabling, following on where they have gone ahead (Luke 10:1): the instinct of team-leader THREE is to remain a member of the team.

In every life there are FOUR moments – moments of separation and pain – and on this basis we see Jesus at FOUR most especially in the temptations in the wilderness and in the garden of Gethsemane. On both occasions he is very much alone, doing battle with fear and temptation, and seeing it all in images, emotions, and dreams: the stones appear like bread; there are visions of Jerusalem and of all the nations of the world; there is the cup of suffering – "let this cup pass from me" – and angels appear to comfort him (Luke 4:1-13; 22:39-46).

The calm way in which Jesus concludes his meeting with the woman caught in adultery (John 8:3-11) could suggest that he actually dealt with this situation more from FOUR than from TWO: he did not so much pity the woman – a TWO response – as empathize with her and all victims like her, as one who was about to be sacrificed himself under the hypocrisy of the supposed guardians of God's law. Certainly throughout the scene Jesus creates a perfect work of art – full of dramatic tension, and with a perfect poetic line at its center: "he stood up tall and said, let the sinless one among you cast the first stone."

FOUR has an eye for beauty as well as a gift for poetry – "consider the lilies of the field" (Matthew 6:28-29) – and FOUR has an eye for the meaningful, dramatic act – like riding into the city on a donkey (Matthew 21:6-10).

The perfect gift of Jesus at FOUR is the institution of the Eucharist. It has everything. It is about pain, deeper than any of us can know, symbolized in broken bread and poured out wine. That pain is converted into the most profound, the most beautiful, the most simple symbolic act, with so many levels of meaning: the gathering, the breaking, the transforming, the sharing, and the uniting; bread for all of our ordinariness, wine for our sorrow and joy; a connection with the Last Supper and the cross in history; a connection with the heavenly banquet still to come; the life and nourishment of the risen Christ in symbols of both death and life, for the people of the resurrection on their journey today. In the Eucharist, pain and suffering, still remembered, are converted into life. It was a gift to the world, and the world has received it. Jesus took bread, gave thanks, broke it, and gave it to them, saying, "this is my body, given for you." He took the cup, gave thanks, and gave it to them, saying, "do this in remembrance of me." And we do – a million times a million times over – and Christ is made present once again. It is the whole of time and eternity's most perfect piece of FOUR.

The FIVE in Jesus seeks time alone to pray – and to think with objectivity. In the wilderness and in Gethsemane, Jesus fought a battle in logic and words as well as in emotions. In Mark 1:35-39, Jesus goes out of the town alone to pray, and there in prayer resolves not to return to those who are seeking him, but to move on to the next town. Jesus commends the strategy of FIVE, to think it through first, for all of his followers, when he mocks those who – metaphorically – start a tower they cannot complete, or begin a battle they can never win (Luke 14:28-33). In Luke 2:40-52 we see Jesus being FIVE at the age of twelve in the temple in Jerusalem, already growing "in both wisdom and stature," taking it all in and thinking it through. The result is that later he teaches with authority, "and not as their scribes" (Matthew 7:28-29).

The loyalty of SIX is seen supremely as Jesus moves toward the cross: "not my will, but thine, be done" (Luke 22:42). The whole story of Jesus' faithfulness to God's plan of salvation is told in Philippians 2:6-11: "Christ Jesus, being in the form of God, did not grasp at equality with God, but emptied himself, taking the form of a slave, being born in human likeness; and being in human form, humbled himself, becoming obedient even to death, to death on a cross. Therefore God highly exalted him, and gave him the name above every name, that at the name of Jesus, every knee should bow, in heaven and on earth and under the earth" – all this through the faithfulness and the loyalty and the courage which is SIX: to cling fast to that which is surely of God, and not let go.

And Jesus even has the wonderful, joyful, humorous light touch of SEVEN. How many fish are caught when the risen Jesus appears at the lakeside? More than strictly necessary – at one hundred and fifty three (John 21:1-14). How much wine at the wedding in Cana in Galilee? More than strictly decent, and good quality as well (John 2:1-11). But how many loaves and fish are available to feed five thousand? The optimist and the generalist say, let's break it up and share it out and see how far we get (John 6:9-13). And there is something about redeemed SEVEN which – like Jesus of Nazareth – has seen all the pain and the sin of the world, and still believes that the kingdom of God is among us (Luke 17:21), still believes in resurrection: still believes that there is hope for us all.

And so it is that uniquely in Jesus we see all nine types, and all nine types perfected: the team leadership of THREE, the courageous loyalty of SIX, and the steadfastness and peacefulness of NINE; the idealism of ONE, the compassion of TWO, the creativity of FOUR, the quiet wisdom of FIVE, the playfulness of SEVEN, and the challenge of EIGHT.

Our calling as individuals is not to be the whole body of Christ complete in ourselves – but each to be one member of the body of Christ. Each brings different gifts and blessings, together making up the completeness of the body of Christ on earth. For each one of us, the perfection of our particular gift is seen in the earthly ministry of Jesus in the Gospels. Each one of us can aspire to Christ-likeness in the gifts we have received. And each one of us can take up a place reserved and ready for us within the living temple of God's church on earth. Every gift is welcome – and every gift is needed to complete the whole.

Part 4

Prayer

Prayer in the three centers

How shall we pray?

It is the question every Christian wants to ask, but no one dares, assuming others will think less of them. But everybody wants to know how. How shall we pray?

The classic models invite us to pray every day – or at the beginning and end of every day – or at several different hours throughout the day. Saint Paul even suggests that we should pray constantly (1 Thessalonians 5:17). But how shall we pray?

The liturgy of the church offers us psalms, and formal written prayers, and readings from the Scriptures and the saints. A classic mnemonic – ACTS – invites us to work through our own extempore Adoration, Confession, Thanksgiving, and prayers of Supplication. So we read these words, or we think through these topics, but is that prayer? How shall we pray?

The perfect prayer takes all that we are and offers it up to God. The perfect prayer takes body and mind and heart, and offers them up to God.

It is the mind that will most easily be caught up into prayer through the use of words. Written words, memorized words, extempore words, can lift the mind to God: words of adoration, words of confession, words of thanksgiving, words of intercession – and the Scriptures, writings, and prayers of the church. By this prayer the mind is offered up to God and transformed.

The heart will most easily pray in images and emotions without any words. The prayer of the heart occurs not when the prayer is spoken in words, but when it is felt in the images and emotions and compassion of the heart. The heart is lifted up to God by choosing to dwell for a precious and silent time in the images and emotions of the adoration of God, in the images and emotions of humble confession before God, in the images and emotions of profound gratitude toward God, and in the images and emotions of the compassionate and trusting plea before God. The heart may often be well guided into these images and emotions by the words of the psalms and the prayers of the church – but will need silence between the words "to do the heart work." Non-verbal images – through any of the five senses – can equally guide the heart to prayer. In either case it is important that the heart should not be overwhelmed or bombarded: it has prayer work to do. By this prayer work in image and compassion and emotion, the heart can be offered up to God, and transformed.

And for some people, neither the mind nor the heart is the center of who they are: both the prayer of the mind and the prayer of the heart seem awkward and artificial, disconnected from the real business of life. These are the gut types, and they really do pray most easily through their bodies: through their hands, through their actions, through their posture, through their resolve, or by just being there. And just as we all need to find both the prayer of the mind and the prayer of the heart if we are to offer our whole selves to God, so also we need to find the prayer that offers up the rest of who we are. At the end of the Eucharist we pray: "we offer you our souls and bodies to be a living sacrifice."

We can pray through our hands: to be doing the right thing can be a form of prayer; to be doing the wrong thing is to be far from prayer. The priest and the Levite who passed by on the other side were missing their opportunity to pray: the practical attention of the Samaritan to the person in need was a worthy form of prayer (Luke 10:29-37). Adoration, confession, thanksgiving, and supplication can all be caught up in the process of that act of kindness – prayer, literally, in action.

We can pray through posture. Sometimes the words and images and emotions mean less than the action of being physically "on our knees" – in adoration or confession or supplication – or on our feet in thanksgiving. There will be times when it is right to experience the peace of God's presence in the complete stillness of our bodies. There will be times when it is right to experience the overwhelming joy of God's presence in dance – if only in the dance of the liturgy: standing to hear the words of Christ proclaimed, greeting our neighbors at the peace, singing to raise the roof, rising to tip toes at the high praise of the eucharistic prayer, forming processions, raising hands, and gathering at the altar for the sharing of broken bread and poured out wine. To experience the sacraments is, supremely, to bring the experience of prayer into our physicality. And sometimes the most important prayer is simply being there, in the place of prayer: the words and the images may not connect, the mind and the heart may be weary, but the body is there, making the sacrifice of praise, humbly offered up to God for God's transformation of purpose, for God's service.

One of these zones of prayer – body or head or heart – will be your home zone, the place you most easily pray – but the perfect prayer takes all that we are and offers it up to God. The perfect prayer takes body and mind and heart, and offers them up to God, "a living sacrifice."

How shall we pray? With body, mind and heart.

Praying for others

Other people are sometimes a mystery – but Jesus bids us to pray for them all, even those we might call our enemies (Matthew 5:44; Luke 6:28).

There may be people around you for whom you find it almost too easy to name the principal sin. All you have ever seen – or all you have ever registered – is the negative side – the corrupt form – of their engagement with yourself and the world.

But the sin reveals the strategy, and the strategy points to the gifts. If you know the sin, you know the vocation: you know God's invitation to that person, their potential place within the body of Christ.

You can hold that knowledge as a sacred trust – and you can hold that trust in your prayers.

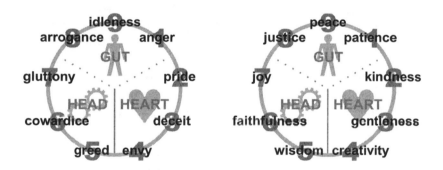

The seven deadly sins

Many have been taught to prepare for confession by reviewing the list of the seven deadly sins.

This concise list, distilled from the Scriptures of the Old Testament and the New, is not a simple list of things that we ought not to do: rather it is an invitation to a far deeper examination of the way we work inside – in our heads, in our hearts, and in our gut reactions.

Seven items is an arbitrary but convenient length for the list: much shorter, and there could be important omissions; much longer, and it could become repetitive. The list of seven is the list we happen to have inherited into the modern age. It is concise and memorable. Seven is fine.

Nine might just be better. There are two good candidates.

To many the list of seven will be familiar already: anger, pride, envy, greed, gluttony, lust, and sloth. Every one of these sins eats away at us from the inside – corrupting our thoughts, our words, and our deeds. We do well to pause from time to time for self-examination, to see whether these sins are eating away at what we could be – at what we could be for God, and for others, and for ourselves – if we were not hindered by habitual sin. Self-examination is the essential first step that can lead on to a resolution to change – to do better by God's grace.

On the list of seven, "greed" – or classically "avarice" – is about hoarding and stinginess, which distinguishes it from "gluttony," also on the list, which is about excessive consumption. And "pride" is not pride in the modern sense of a basic, moderate, healthy self-esteem – something Jesus positively encouraged in the lowly and oppressed – but the sin of a self-absorbed self-importance; the pride that comes before a fall.

Lust is an interesting case. When Jesus said at the Last Supper that he had "earnestly desired" to eat this Passover with his disciples (Luke 22:15) he used the same word that he used when he condemned the man who looks on a woman with "earnest desire" – or "lust" (Matthew 5:28). But Jesus' "earnest desire" for the Last Supper is not a sin – and neither, in itself, is sexuality. The sin is the arrogance that reduces another to the status of an object. The sin of "lust" is not the sexuality but the arrogance. The sin of arrogance deserves to be on the list in its own right – more aggressive and outwardly focused than the self-absorbed self-importance of pride – and it is on the list, as the item that is classically rendered as "lust."

The sin of cowardice would be a valid addition to the list. Cowardice is the opposite of loyalty and faithfulness. God wants people who will march onward into God's promised land – not wander forever in fear in the wilderness.

And those in power, the masters of spin, have always been prone to the sin of deceit – not just lies but a whole tangle of falsehoods. Perhaps that is why such an obvious wrong as deceit was easy to drop when reducing the list to a concise and practical seven.

And so the nine deadly sins are these: the arrogance of EIGHT, the idleness of NINE, the anger of ONE, the pride of TWO, the deceit of THREE, the envy of FOUR, the avarice or greed or hoarding stinginess of FIVE, the cowardice of SIX, and the gluttony of SEVEN.

Admitting the home base temptation can be the hardest thing, but it is the sin most likely to be eating us away, preventing us from moving on. Recognizing it, naming it, and confronting it, can be the first step toward a new place and a new life. When you feel yourself losing your grip, you can pause and say to yourself, "deal with the …" – and name your temptation. In that simple act you reorient yourself – literally "turn around" or "repent" – away from your sin, and toward your potential.

Confession and resolution

The contemporary forms of "general confession," drawn from ancient principles, ring true for everyone: that we have done wrong, against God and neighbor, in thought and word and deed, and in what we have left undone.

In the great outpouring of new liturgical resources in the present day, many modern confessions fail to hit the mark for most readers. They use images and words for misdeeds and imperfections which sound like somebody else's particular neurosis, not yours: you can imagine their writers meaning every word, but they leave you the reader thinking "speak for yourself!" – and they fail to touch what it is that you do need humbly to bring before God that day.

The pattern of the nine types makes sense of this experience. The classic principles of the general confession ring true for us all, but so much else is specific to the patterns of interaction with the world which follow from the strategy – the temptations and energies and hopes and fears which belong distinctively to each of the nine types.

The nine modern "confessions" which follow are complete spiritual exercises in themselves. They are very complete: they confess every detail of the sinful, broken, and imperfect lives that we live. There is one for each of the nine types in turn.

The process of confession as part of prayer can uncover things you would rather keep hidden – but the purpose is healing and forgiveness in the presence of our gracious God. These nine type-specific confessions are uncannily perceptive: they do "hit the mark." These confessions may take you to places you would rather not go – places you have never been or places you left behind long ago – but their purpose is healing and forgiveness on the journey from corruption to redemption. Many will not be for you – but one or more may be your confession, and a gateway, by God's grace, toward redemption.

These nine confessions were created by Éilís Bergin and the late Eddie Fitzgerald. They are presented here with only minor alterations, with the kind permission of their publishers, SDB Media in Dublin.

Each confession concludes with a resolution – an expression of resolve – which moves from the singular – "I" – to the plural – "we" – placing the reader in solidarity with all those other Christian people who share their journey and their type.

Confession at EIGHT

I am EIGHT. Deep down I'm arrogant. That's my brokenness. Pleasure for me is bound up with control. I exploit people because of my passion to dominate and possess. I violate their space, use them without shame, and humiliate them without guilt. At my worst I simply don't consider how vulnerable people can be and have no respect for their feelings. I satisfy my instincts and enjoy life's pleasures without too many hang-ups. I can be cruel rather than kind. Sometimes I punish people disproportionately for the mistakes that they have made. When I put forward high standards of morality I expect others to live up to them without really feeling obliged to do so myself.

I like to keep tabs on things, to check up on even the most trivial details. It's my way of not letting things get out of hand. I value my independence and prefer to be dominant in my relationships. I'm very possessive and I find it hard to compromise or adapt. I tend to bully people and I don't respect those who will not fight back. I see things in black and white. People are either for me or against me, friends or enemies.

Without realizing it, I find myself pushing people around. I'm generally insensitive to the hurt I'm causing. I substitute aggressive behavior for playfulness and sexual activity for intimacy. I have no problem about fighting "dirty." I'm direct, often to the point of rudeness, and use strong language to emphasize what I'm trying to say. I don't pull my punches. I say what I mean and mean what I say. I tend to confront rather than communicate. I readily spit out my anger in the belief that attack is the best form of defense.

Lord God, I know you have given me an enormous passion for life, for love, and for justice. It comes out in the way I generally take the side of the underdog. But I have to avoid becoming a self-appointed judge and jury, always willing to retaliate when I think the balance needs to be redressed. I have to accept my vulnerability and let others see the tender and more gentle side of me, which I keep so well hidden beneath my deliberately tough exterior.

We are EIGHTs. Our inner journey demands an openness to God and to other people. We need to strive to integrate action and contemplation, and to balance our contrary instincts of passionate expression and the refusal of self-disclosure. Since we generally live in the present we find it easy to be immediately present to God in prayer. For us this involves a centering of ourselves, an emptying of thoughts and feelings, a letting go of activity, and a stillness of loving presence which transcends our everyday wants and needs. As gut people we naturally want to be doing and are suspicious of inactivity. But our best prayer is that of simple presence. Paradoxically it brings us both a heightened sensitivity and a calming inner tranquility.

Confession at NINE

I am NINE. Deep down I'm slothful. That's my brokenness. I don't even bother to try to cover it up. There's no need to, since I have effectively persuaded myself and everybody else that I'm just easy-going. But the truth is that I try to avoid all conflict and I am prepared to settle for peace at any price. To avoid facing problems I tend to sweep them under the carpet, denying that they exist – and make molehills out of mountains to soften the pain. I regularly settle for less.

Basically, I'm cynical about human nature. I see nobody as a big deal, not even myself. I have a poor self-image and I am not convinced of my own significance.

The core of my laziness probably lies in my belief that nothing really matters, and that consequently there's no great harm in taking the path of least resistance. I much prefer to get on with the bits and pieces rather than the things that demand responsibility and commitment. It is hard for me to make decisions and I tend to procrastinate. I regularly put off difficult tasks and become vague or obstinate when people try to pin me down. My lack of response is a form of passive aggression, which I find very effective. Because I'm not a self-starter I'm inclined to be addictive. I generally have to look for stimulation outside of myself.

Lord God, I've spent my life trying to deny my feelings. I've attempted to shut them down to avoid the pain they bring. This is how I try to control my environment and gain some power over the ebb and flow of my life. I am prone to inertia. I'm afraid of being overwhelmed by uncontrollable emotions. In particular, I swallow my anger and let it fester within. Help me to accept my emotions and allow my gut feelings to surface and give me life.

We are NINEs. We disconnect so well from unhelpful emotions that we sometimes lose our own special gift: to connect with the beauty, the intensity, and the thrill of the present. When we over-value being calm and peaceful the danger is that we find it difficult to become excited or enthusiastic about anything. We have to stop putting ourselves down and continually defining ourselves in terms of what we think others expect of us. Deepening our awareness that we are loved by God precisely for who we are can help us become more self-confident and independent. We will not then feel so overwhelmed by life's difficulties. Instead of withdrawing from the scene, we will become actively involved, determining our priorities and accepting responsibility for the decisions we make.

Confession at ONE

I am ONE. Deep down I'm angry. That's my brokenness. I don't normally admit this. I generally cover it up so that nobody knows. But the tenseness of my body, in particular my face, often betrays me. I have a very strong sense of right and wrong and an inner voice criticizes me when I fail. I don't want to be seen as a hypocrite. I do so want to measure up to what God expects of me. The trouble is that I also want to achieve the impossibly high standards I frequently set for myself. And because I don't, I am fundamentally angry – at God for not making me perfect in the first place, at others for contributing to the mess the world is in, and at myself for not arriving more rapidly at what I consider to be spiritual wholeness. Time just runs away from me and I think I'll never make it.

I always want to live from strength, not weakness. I like the strength I find in a spirituality of self-control. But then I dislike the cold shell I seem to have constructed – because it makes it difficult for others to get to know me, and gives the impression that I am dismissive of people. I built it to protect myself from getting hurt, and to prevent others from seeing that I bleed too.

I can see the faults in everything and everyone – and it has made me judgmental, critical, and negative. Only grudgingly and with deliberate effort am I a source of affirmation and praise. Nobody else seems to care passionately about things the way that I do. It feels like they take my efforts for granted – and I resent that. I often think that when I share what little goodness I have, I just waste it.

Lord God, there are times when I look at myself and see only a sinner and you as a just judge who will make me pay for all my imperfections. I know that both of these are inadequate and that in reality you are wonderfully compassionate, and you choose to see me as good – as forgiven. I just need to be patient: to do what I can, and then to wait for the growth that comes through your healing touch.

We are ONEs. Allowing God to work in us, to heal our anger and ease our pain is a life-long process. We mustn't be impatient or want everything "now." A spirituality which is strongly influenced by social justice issues is attractive to our type, given our interest in putting things right and transforming the mess – but the quiet, gentle approach is often what we need the most. This is all the more important since we experience the world as being bigger than we are. It follows that we feel we have to work harder to control our environment and set things right. When we let God be God and stop taking upon ourselves the burden of single-handedly trying to improve on creation, we will save ourselves a lot of needless distress.

Confession at TWO

I am TWO. Deep down I'm proud. That's my brokenness. I feel I'm better than others because I'm generally more caring. I see the needs of others even before they do themselves and do everything I can to help them, sometimes without even being asked. I constantly put myself out to be of service, but I also expect people to recognize and appreciate what I do for them.

However, when I really think about it, I know that my helpfulness is both a source of recognition and a way of seeing myself as being of value. I know that what appears to others as selfless and generous is not entirely so. There are often strings attached. I exercise pressure indirectly and by stealth. I don't blatantly seek to manipulate, but I know that what I do is manipulative nonetheless. Being helpful is my way of getting attention, of asking for love without putting it into words. It feels good to have people who depend on me. Their need gives me a sense of being important, useful, and worthwhile. It helps me define who I am.

Lord God, I know this means I don't have a good self-image, and that I don't appreciate the gift you have given me. You love me unconditionally. I don't have to keep proving myself, to you or to anyone else. I don't have to try so hard to please all the time. Love cannot be earned or paid for. It is always a gift. Help me to realize that the needs I perceive in others are often a reflection of those within myself. Give me the humility to accept that I, too, am in need of help.

We are TWOs. Our constant concern for others frequently masks the lack of attention we pay to our own physical, emotional, and spiritual needs. We help others and we neglect ourselves. But if we're always giving, always active, is there anything for ourselves when at some point we stop the treadmill? Who fills the emptiness of our personal storehouse? We need to learn the spiritual truth that "charity begins at home," that without a realistic acceptance of our own woundedness, we cannot even begin to understand the pain of others – let alone help them through it. We need the humility to accept our brokenness, and the patience to allow God's love to heal our wounds.

Confession at THREE

I am THREE. Deep down I'm deceitful. That's my brokenness. I cover it up so that it's even hidden from myself. I'm radically out of touch with my innermost depths of feeling and love. I keep myself constantly busy so as not to have to face my real self. I am skilled at covering up, at showing a different face for every possible occasion. Pretence comes naturally to me, as I strive to be a winner in everything I do.

I court success, security, and prestige because I'm afraid of failure. I don't stop long enough to face the truth behind the masks of my own making. I know I need to learn the success of apparent failure and the failure of what sometimes looks like success. I need to absorb the lesson of the cross, the glory of failure, the economy of grace.

I'm ever restless, always on the move, never still. I prefer to be a moving target rather than a sitting duck. I give the impression that I have it made, that everything comes so easily to me. But in reality, I'm living a lie.

Lord God, there are times when I see myself as a superficial shell, and you as the successful creator with whom I long to compete. You created me in your image – and yet I have spent much of my life trying to embellish it to my own liking, hiding your beautiful handiwork under a constant series of masks. You are interested in the reality, not in the substitute image. You see the human vulnerable face behind my high-profile, self-sufficient mask. And you love me in spite of my duplicity and image-making. Help me to get in touch with my need for others, with the tender side of my heart, and with the truth beyond the soft option and the hard sell. Show me that what I achieve in worldly terms is as nothing to the generosity of your passionate love. My life is lived at a frenetic pace, but you see the still center where my heart aches and I crave for love. Slow me down, Lord, so that I can know – with a calm heart – the real secret of creative love.

We are THREEs. Risking the self-revelation and self-giving of love takes time. Our defenses have been built up over many years. Deceit is not healed in a day. The very failures we experience as we grow into truthfulness should encourage us that we are moving in the direction of wholeness. We love to be seen to be doing things – but we need to know who we are: to find the balance between doing and being.

Confession at FOUR

I am FOUR. Deep down I'm envious. That's my brokenness. I'm usually too ashamed or too caught up in my own feelings to admit this. I'm so afraid of the pain of rejection. I long to be special, to be different, somehow to rise above the ordinary and the mundane. I am especially sensitive to beauty in all its forms. I love anything that is simple, natural, authentic. My standards are so high that the more I try to reach them, the more artificial I become. I can't help comparing myself with people who have more talent, taste, sophistication, and class than I have, and longing to be somehow superior.

I envy them the ease with which they seem to live their lives. It's easier for me to live in memories, dreams, and the world of the arts than in the everyday world, where the mess is part of the reality. I have real problems with intimacy and distance. What I have, I don't value; what I long for, I treasure. I'm regularly disappointed by life and I live with a deep sense of loss. Why do others seem to have it all? Even in my relationships I'm jealous of others being somehow more interesting or attractive than I am. I'm ashamed of my body, my inner turmoil torments me, and I regularly run myself down.

Lord God, all of this causes me intense inner suffering. I go through a roller-coaster of feelings, from ecstatic joy to inexpressible sadness. People think this is just moodiness. If only they knew how deep it goes, they'd see what a dreadful burden it is.

Life is such a struggle for me, Lord, yet I'm tragically unwilling to accept help. Please help me. Help me to appreciate the special sensitivity you have given me – the ability to understand at depth the emotional life of others. Show me how to be realistic enough not to imagine this world as the safe haven of my dreams, but as holding in balance tears and laughter, pain and joy, ugliness and beauty, violence and peace. Help me not to be so elitist, so snobbish, but to value the normal, the ordinary, and the everyday.

We are FOURs. For us the movement is from the romanticized memories of the past and the hoped-for visions of the future to the humdrum reality of the present. We need to learn to be at ease and content with the way things are, understanding that "God is in the pots and pans," that we meet God in the ordinary, the everyday, the mundane, the pedestrian, the hackneyed. Rather than bemoan people's misunderstanding of who we are, we should try to use our talents of empathy, communication, and creativity to create a voice for the things of the heart – for all.

Confession at FIVE

I am FIVE. Deep down I'm greedy – not so much for material things as for the knowledge that will give meaning to my life. That's my brokenness. I find it hard to admit this, even to myself, and I have the skills to cover it up so that nobody knows. But the truth is that I'm so afraid of feeling empty inside that I continually long for fulfillment. I dread the idea of meaninglessness and my continual quest for knowledge is simply my way of dealing with this.

Sometimes I experience such great loneliness that the only way I can feel safe is to shut myself away, most frequently by living inside my head. I appear confident and self-assured on the surface, but deep down I experience a great deal of insecurity. I attempt to fill the void with many things, to no avail – and yet I don't like intrusions and I am very protective of my own space.

I generally try to remain calm and keep my emotions under control. When I'm angry, upset, fearful, or emotional, I try not to show it. But I do feel things deeply. It's just that I tend to analyze my feelings rather than immediately experience them. I find it hard to express my emotions or put them into words. It's much easier for me to show warmth toward friends who are absent than those who are present.

Lord God, you know me better than I do myself. You know how difficult it is for me to trust other people, to let go of my fortress mentality, to avoid being cynical. I consider myself superior to others because I think I'm perceptive enough to see through their superficiality and sham. But the loss is mine, not theirs. I've lost the common touch because of my tendency to over-analyze everything.

Lord, I know I'm not the "giving" sort. I certainly find it very painful to get involved. I both long for and somehow feel threatened by intimacy. I don't look for attention and don't allow others the opportunity for making demands on me. I limit my contacts with people and compartmentalize my life precisely in order to avoid involvement. I prefer to retreat or intellectualize rather than get "stuck in." Help me to become the person who meets with others and gives open-handedly from the wealth of resources I have collected, rather than hoarding them and venturing out only to collect more.

We are FIVEs. Our spiritual journey is from the internal to the external. It involves taking the incarnation seriously. It means accepting that knowledge comes through the heart and the senses as well as through the head. The fact is that God became flesh, not newsprint, and there's no escaping the implications of that. Unfortunately, there is a painful split within us between theory and practice, between contemplation and action. We must be bold enough to risk involvement, and inventive enough to give practical expression to our insights and reflections. Then we will not give in to disengagement, and others will be able to share in the wisdom we have to bring.

Confession at SIX

I am SIX. Deep down I'm fearful. That's my brokenness. I'm not willing to admit it, but it comes out in my doubts and in my deeply anxious approach to life. I am very mistrustful – of myself and others. I seem to be continually watchful and afraid. My self-doubt and lack of self-confidence makes me much too dependent on others, particularly on those in a position of authority. Relying on tradition, the law, and the institutions of society gives me a great sense of security and helps allay my fear of making a mistake.

I find it difficult to trust my own abilities and instincts. Yet, at the same time, I do not completely trust others. I can spot danger a mile off and I am quick to look for cover. I prefer to see things in straightforward terms, in black and white rather than shades of gray. I like to be sure of my position and not contradict myself. I pay attention to detail – and then I find it hard to make up my mind. I either hesitate and allow myself to be led by others, or I over-compensate, become obstinate and defiant, and take risks.

Even though I work well in a group, the model I work out of is hierarchical. There is a sense in which my loyalty to the group is just an expression of my basic insecurity – a way of finding strength in numbers. I don't really have the courage of my own convictions. Indeed, my sense of duty is often a cover for my anxiety about making decisions for myself. What it amounts to is a fear of freedom, a fundamental unwillingness to say "yes" or "no" on my own.

Lord God, what I need is faith in you and in my own goodness. I find it difficult to accept undiluted praise because I don't really believe in my own value and worth. But you have given me a wonderful variety of talents and gifts, and called me into your close circle of friends.

Help me to realize, Lord, that you do not expect impossible standards from me. Give me the faith to believe that you love me for who I am. Give me the courage to take responsibility for my day-to-day choices. Help me to give myself permission to own my feelings and to open myself up to you and others in a relationship of trust and intimacy.

We are SIXes. Our spiritual journey is from self-protective assessment to courageous commitment. We make our choices and then commit to them – with faithfulness and loyalty and even a kind of confidence – but we have to focus more on making those choices and making them well. We cannot keep backing out of life, refusing to make decisions or move on for fear of what might go wrong. True discipleship involves costly action. Trust in God means facing our fear of the unfamiliar, the unknown and the unexpected – and then stepping out in trust.

Confession at SEVEN

I am SEVEN. Deep down I'm intemperate. That's my brokenness. I don't normally admit it, but I'm a glutton for more. What I want is a superabundance of the good things in life, of the things that are likely to bring me happiness. Nothing is ever enough. I consume things rather than savor and enjoy them. I take life in big gulps rather than in little sips. I emphasize the positive and minimize the negative. Basically, what I'm doing is trying to avoid pain and the emptiness inside.

Even though I move around a lot, essentially I live in my head. I always concentrate on the good, and rationalize or trivialize the difficult: I have lots of plans and schemes for doing good, but I gloss over the problems. I'm future-orientated, always anticipating life. The fact that I don't fully experience the pleasure of the present leads to my not being completely satisfied. I generally make sure I have so much to do that I'll never get bored. Indeed, my need for constant stimulation leads me, at times, to addictive behavior.

I look for distractions to keep me occupied and help me cope with painful realities. I find it hard to delay gratification. When I want things I want them now. My senses are so sharp that I can almost taste the enjoyment. The trouble is that I can also vividly imagine the intensity of pain, and I look for every possible diversion to avoid it. That's why I'm continually on the go and try not to get tied down to routine tasks. In effect, I'm running away from myself because I fear that if I stop to look inside I won't like what I see.

Lord God, slow me down long enough to discover the depth and beauty within. You have given me a childlike wonder at life, the blessing of good humor, and a marvelous sense of fun. I am able to see the ridiculous side of life and make people laugh. That's a precious commodity in today's world. But I need help to realize that I do not have to search for happiness non-stop – that if I cease my restless pursuit of it, happiness will surely find me. I need to discover that real joy is not dependent on outside circumstances but lies essentially within my own heart. Help me to dig beneath the surface so as to gain the true perspective of depth.

We are SEVENs. We need to become more reflective and responsible on the inside – and more honestly engaged with the realities outside. Our natural curiosity and our attraction to constant change and the "quick fix" make it very difficult for us to focus our attention when we come to pray. There are so many delightful possibilities and options to choose from, that given the opportunity, we attempt to pursue them all. However, we can slow down our mental games by "anchoring" ourselves in the real – perhaps beginning by adopting a posture which ensures a rare stillness: then we can begin.

Daily prayer

These short prayers, one for each of the nine types, can help us to focus daily on the blessings and the challenges of being who we are. Lest we forget, they give thanks daily for the gifts God has given. They offer to God all that we are, as we are, and they pray that God will help us to grow daily in our calling. At least one of them is yours. Others may be perfect gifts for people you know.

Once again, they are adapted from originals by Éilís Bergin and Eddie Fitzgerald, with the kind permission of their publishers, SDB Media.

Daily prayer for EIGHT

Lord God, I thank you
for giving me a tremendous passion for life,
a powerful sense of justice,
and the energy to get things done.
Help me always to protect the weak
and champion the oppressed –
and give me a heart filled with compassion,
that I might know the strength that comes through gentleness
and the respect that comes through love.

Daily prayer for NINE

Lord God, I thank you
for giving me a profound peace of heart and mind
and a simple trust in the goodness of creation.
Help me to know that you have a chosen place for me,
in your heart, and in your purposes for the world.
Help me to keep my energy and direction
to live the gift of each day to the full.

(MH)

Daily prayer for ONE

Lord God, I thank you
for giving me a keen sense of what is right,
and a diligent desire to do good.
In my attempts to live up to my ideals,
help me to be patient and forgiving.
Teach me to be tolerant of mistakes
rather than always finding fault.
Show me how to accept what is good enough,
and above all how to lighten up, enjoy life,
and gently relax in your love.

Daily prayer for TWO

Lord God, I thank you
for giving me the gift of a generous heart.
Help me to understand that your love and care for me
do not depend on what I do for others.
Show me how to minister to the needs of others
without losing sight of my own needs;
and allow me to feel in my own wounds
the healing power of your love.

Daily prayer for THREE

Lord God, I thank you
for giving me the heart
to bring hope and encouragement
to any situation.
Give me the grace to work with others
with humility and gentleness and respect.
Help me always to be open and honest
with myself, with others, and with you,
that my purposes may be your purposes,
and my commitment may be to you alone.

(MH)

Daily prayer for FOUR

Lord God, I thank you
for giving me a keen eye for beauty,
and a special sensitivity to the human heart.
Show me how even the most ordinary things
are filled with the wonder of your presence.
Help me to live in the present moment
and to appreciate that my tears and laughter, joy and pain,
are part of your loving plan for the world.

Daily prayer for FIVE

Lord God, I thank you for giving me the gifts
of insight and discernment
as I look out on the wonders of the created world.
Help me to trust in the wisdom and goodness
of your plans for your creation.
Give me the generosity to share what I have with others,
and the courage to involve myself directly
in their daily cares and concerns.
Above all, give me the confidence to go where you would lead,
and the peace to trust in you.

(adapted)

Daily prayer for SIX

Lord God, I thank you for giving me the gifts
of faithfulness to your calling
and fellowship among your people.
Help me to understand more fully
the true depth of your love for me,
and the breadth of your love for the world.
Safe in the knowledge of your love,
and relying on your tender care,
may I have the courage to overcome my fears,
and the confidence to go where you would lead –
trusting in your generous compassion for us all.

(adapted)

Daily prayer for SEVEN

Lord God, I thank you for giving me the gifts
of gratitude and joy in the present
and hope and trust for the future.
May they be fixed so deep within my heart
that I may greet even the challenges and tears of the present
with the openness and compassion
which come from a trust in your perfect goodness
and a knowledge of your perfect care.

(MH)

The Lord's Prayer

The Lord's Prayer has a special place in the life of the Christian community. For centuries it has stood both as the prayer which unites us all when we meet together, and as the prayer which draws together all of our prayers when we recite it alone. Line by line, it gathers up all that we are. Line by line, it draws in the whole community: it is there for us all, and it needs us all.

Our Father...

The prayer draws us together in its very first line. In saying "Our Father," we seek to be people who belong easily to one another, with no barriers between us: one people united before God, at peace with God and one another. This first line calls us together into the place of prayer – the loving presence of our God. It comes from a peaceful and trusting place within us that reaches out directly to God, in fellowship with one another. As an entry into prayer it is open and unselfconscious. "Our Father" is a line that belongs to the gut zone – and ultimately to NINE. This is the line that draws in NINE, and draws in that peaceful, open, and unselfconscious place in every one of us – and the gifts of sector NINE live out its meaning.

...who art in heaven

Location matters to the gut and to the gut types: place – groundedness – is important. But information about location is not the purpose of this line. Consider the richness which is missed if this line is omitted: we would be taking out a reference to heaven, the place of perfection – perfect love, perfect beauty, perfect wisdom, perfect safety, perfect peace, perfect joy, the perfection of all God's creation – the place of every perfected ideal. "Who art in heaven...": it is whispered in awe; it is all about perfected ideals. It belongs to ONE – and to that gut-and-heart place in every one of us.

Hallowed be thy name

This line is a small offering of adoration. Again, imagine the prayer without it: without this line, the prayer lacks worship, and feels mechanical and cold. This is the Christian's whisper of love to the God of compassionate care. It springs from the love in the Christian soul, one to one, for God. It is the loving prayer of TWO – and of that heart-and-gut place in everyone.

Thy kingdom come

There is a central place in Jesus' teaching for the kingdom: the kingdom of heaven or the kingdom of God, growing like a mustard seed, leavening the dough, already among us and yet still to come. The journey toward the kingdom is the shared adventure into which we are called: it is an adventure of fellowship and community, of sharing gifts and supporting one another, of promoting the weak and sharing the gifts of the strong, of being one active, moving, supportive team with one goal – to be living within God's purposes. Among us are those whom God has gifted to help hold this fellowship together, inspiring and encouraging, turning a crowd into a kingdom: God's kingdom, when they work for God alone. Let THREEs redeemed proclaim their vision: "Thy kingdom come" – and let the heart in every one of us seek to capture and share in that vision of what could be.

Thy will be done on earth as it is in heaven

Another mention of heaven – only this time it is all about this project to establish heaven on earth: to see God's will done on earth, to see the unsurpassed splendor and beauty of heaven right here on earth. Among us are those who long to bring a glimpse of heaven into our imperfect world – who paint the beauty of heaven onto the rough canvas of this world. FOURs – and that heart-and-head place in every one of us – speak your prayer: may God's will be done, "on earth as it is in heaven."

Give us this day our daily bread

Enough, you folks from the heart side – idealists and lovers and inspirers and dreamers. Now is the time to think this through. Now is the time to be practical if we are to begin this journey together, rather than merely dream. There will be difficult times. There will be challenges. And there will be the ordinary stuff of daily life. We need practical resources for the journey: nothing too greedy, the basics will do. Bread: we shall need daily bread – or literally "bread for tomorrow." Give us this day our bread for tomorrow. This is redeemed FIVE – and that head-plus-heart place in every one of us: not fearful, not greedy, not hoarding – just practical and wise. Give us what we need on your adventure, O God: "Give us this day our daily bread."

**And forgive us our trespasses,
as we forgive those who trespass against us**

In the objective and rational logic of our heads, we know when we have "trespassed" – and we know when others have trespassed against us. Among us are those for whom the head is very clearly the primary resource – and they observe these trespasses with clarity: drawing their boundaries starkly, they know when they have transgressed, and they know when others have transgressed against them. "Forgive us our trespasses," says SIX, feeling this plea so deeply. And then, with open heart and open hands – kindling all of SIX's fears but so in line with God's will – "...as we forgive those who trespass against us." SIX and the head lead the way in this prayer – and the head and heart and gut of every one of us must surely follow.

Lead us not into temptation, but deliver us from evil

We are surrounded by simply too many temptations, and too much pain – or so it feels to that head-gut place in each one of us, and especially to SEVEN; so "lead us not into temptation," and deliver us from all that would cause pain.

**For thine is the kingdom,
the power, and the glory, for ever and ever**

Another mention for God's kingdom – only this time it is all about eternal glory and power. EIGHT is the one who understands where power lies and what power means. EIGHT, and the gut-plus-head place in every one of us, proclaims where the true power and glory lie – bowing in acknowledgment and adoration: "Thine is the kingdom, the power, and the glory, for ever and for ever."

Amen.

"Amen" – or "we assent," or "let it be so." "Amen": it gathers all of the people, and the whole of the prayer, together in this one word – a perfect concluding moment of unity and peace. In this concluding moment of stillness, the whole community and the whole prayer reach out silently to God: this breath of a word belongs to NINE, welcoming us back to the central place of stillness and unity and peace. Let NINE and the people say: "Amen."

This prayer begins in our "guts," in our createdness, in our direct engagement with the world and with our creator – and it completes a circuit of all that we are: through the passions and emotions and dreams of the heart; through the wisdom and faithfulness and choices of the mind; and back to base, back to the center of our createdness, our wholeness, our being. This one prayer offers to God all that we are – all that we find within ourselves. It offers all of our temptations, all of our gifts, every part of what it means to be human. It offers the parts of our humanity that we understand the most, and the parts of our humanity that we are yet to explore or fully understand. It embraces the whole of our present – all that we are – and the whole of our journey – past and still to come – and offers it all to God.

In a gathering of the Christian community, this prayer moves among the people like a wave. Everyone has a contribution to make, to make the prayer complete. Everyone has their special offering, their particular gift, in this prayer which unites us all – which draws us all in and makes us all one. In this prayer, everyone is needed – everyone has a role. In community or in solitude, this is our prayer.

Appendix 1

The Enneagram

The enneagram – introduction

Part of the structure of the strategy board is the pattern of nine lines within the outer circle – the pattern of nine "well-trodden paths" across the board. This diagram with nine arrows connecting nine points on a circle is the one part of the structure properly know as "the enneagram" – or "nine-pattern." It has some fascinating properties which are well worth examination – and which can add to our understanding of the workings of the strategy board.

The enneagram is a tool for examining the properties of certain three-part systems. It comes in two forms: the static enneagram and the cyclical enneagram.

The cyclical enneagram – "the enneagram of cyclical processes" – introduces a sense of clockwise motion around the outer circumference of the diagram. There was a hint of this in our examination of The Lord's Prayer.

But for the most part, the strategy board has been a "static" system – there has been no particular sense of clockwise or anti-clockwise movement around the outer circle – so we examine first "the static enneagram."

The static enneagram

The enneagram is a remarkably powerful tool for analyzing all kinds of systems where contrasting concepts interact – like head and heart on the strategy board.

Identifying the two major contrasting concepts in the system is the first part of the enneagram analysis. The two contrasting concepts are placed side by side on the diagram – one on the left and one on the right.

In a complex system the concepts will interact in a variety of different ways.

At any given time, one may be significantly stronger than the other, dominating the system – or the two may be closely balanced.

If they are closely balanced, it may be that they are both acting strongly – and this "double action" will have various consequences for the system as a whole. Or it may be that they are finely balanced because they have met in some kind of moderating neutral territory – a place of compromise or pragmatism or complementarity – and this will have a different set of consequences for the system as a whole.

Identifying this distinctive neutral territory – this moderating place – is the next part of the analysis. This place has a significant role of its own as a third element in the system – like the gut zone on the strategy board.

The three "elements" of the system – two contrasting concepts and a distinctive neutral place – are now arranged as three zones in a circular diagram.

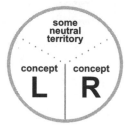

The outer circle of the diagram now represents the different ways in which the three elements of the system can interact.

Nine different patterns of interaction are identified – and represented as nine points on the outer circle.

In some cases, one of the three elements in the system dominates, and the other two elements – if they are present at all – are closely balanced. This is represented here by the darker points on the outer circle.

In other cases, one of the three elements in the system still dominates, but the two remaining elements are not equally balanced. These cases are represented here by the lighter points on the outer circle.

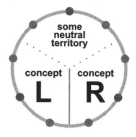

For convenience only, the points are arbitrarily numbered, with the largest number at the top, like a clock face.

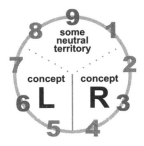

Taking an overview of the whole diagram, point NINE is understood as the central, neutral, moderating place - the essence of the third element in the system.

Points THREE and SIX are called "energy points" or "shock points" which energize the system. The "energy" at point THREE is the essence of concept R, and the "energy" at point SIX is the essence of concept L.

Down at the foot of the diagram, at FIVE and FOUR, the original contrasting concepts are both strong – and they interact strongly, without the moderating influence of the neutral territory at the top of the diagram. They may overlap or merge or "meet at the extremes" – but one of the two always has "the upper hand," so at any given moment the interaction is represented by either point FOUR or point FIVE.

The THREE-SIX-NINE triangle now highlights the three interacting elements in the system – the "neutral place" at the top of the diagram, and the original contrasting concepts at the two "energy points" – suggesting possible links or moves between these three distinctive places.

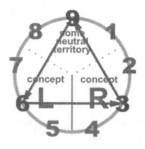

This is the "triangle of simplicity," as each of the three points of the triangle represents the "simple essence" of one element of the system.

Six more lines connect the six points where elements of the system are interacting with each other. This is the "hexagon of complexity" – suggesting other potential links or moves within the system.

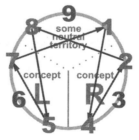

Four of these connecting lines go up and down the two sides of the diagram. They suggest changes of balance between the extreme of each concept at the foot of the diagram and the neutral place at the top of the diagram. They do not cross from one side to the other – from one concept to the other.

The other two lines cross the top of the diagram, suggesting links or moves from one concept to the other – something made possible only by way of the distinctive neutral territory at the top of the diagram.

We now have a graphical representation of the potential interactions between two contrasting concepts and a neutral place.

This "graphical representation" can become "a picture worth a thousand words" when analyzing systems where contrasting concepts interact.

The enneagram of heat and cold

A fairly neutral example for illustration would be an enneagram of the effects of heat and cold.

This quick analysis considers heat and cold as human experiences, rather than points on a precise scale of Celsius or Fahrenheit.

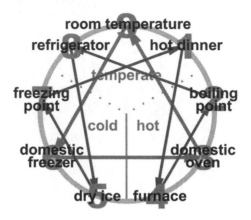

The domestic freezer and the domestic oven can be placed on the diagram as the "energy points," being common and distinctive human experiences of the two contrasting concepts – heat and cold.

Room temperature can be the central, neutral, "temperate" place.

The rare extremes are added at the foot of the diagram, at FIVE and FOUR: the extreme cold of dry ice and the extreme heat of a furnace.

At EIGHT and SEVEN on the cold side, between room temperature and the freezer, are the refrigerator – cool but not freezing – and freezing point itself.

At ONE and TWO on the hot side, between room temperature and the oven, are a hot dinner, and boiling point.

We can now "read off" some of the observations from this simple analysis.

In their effects on the human being, heat and cold do indeed meet at the extremes: they are both highly destructive – they both produce "burns" – so FOUR and FIVE are indeed natural if contrasting neighbors. Moving up the diagram, SIX and THREE can both be painful, but they are safe enough to insulate and keep in the kitchen. For eating and drinking, our outer limits would be ice cream at SEVEN and hot tea at TWO. Less extreme are cool salads at EIGHT and hot dinners at ONE – completing a top-to-bottom scale which has a left-right symmetry of contrasts.

The arrows could then represent actions that we take. The THREE-SIX-NINE triangle represents a simple domestic arrangement, while modern industrial-scale catering uses the other lines on the diagram. The rapid cook-chill system takes ONE – a hot meal – very precisely to SEVEN – freezing point – and not beyond. This produces something like a supermarket microwave ready-meal. In the distribution system this drifts toward EIGHT – ordinary refrigeration temperature. A deliberate shift directly from EIGHT to TWO – "piping hot" – then makes it safe and ready for consumption. On the industrial scale, this process of moves on the hexagon is controlled by extremes beyond domestic norms: it is controlled, in effect, by FIVE and FOUR.

This quick analysis shows how the system works: now to some more significant examples.

The enneagram of retail road vehicles

The example of retail road vehicles began as a humorous observation about the vehicles on the road – but it opened up into a fascinating new area of study, as we shall see.

In the "middle market," and filling most of the lot, are examples of the general-purpose family saloon. It will pack in the luggage for the holiday, or pick up some light furniture, or take waste to the dump, when required – and it will hurry through the traffic when absolutely necessary. But most of the time it is just an ordinary, general purpose, "non-specialist" family vehicle: all the different requirements are "moderated" to fit together on one set of wheels.

Elsewhere on the lot there are two highly specialized alternatives on sale: we might call them "sporty" and "utility." On the right – at point THREE – the compact open-top two-seater. On the left – at point SIX – the practical and functional Land Rover or pick-up truck.

On the forecourt there will also be two interesting alternative models based on that standard saloon: the "estate car" version, with much more space for carrying larger loads, and the discretely "tuned up" version, with a range of small improvements to the performance of the engine and the brakes and the gears. These are the general-purpose vehicles with utility or sporty influences: they go on the diagram at EIGHT and ONE.

You will also find a vehicle which will seat five and which does have some storage space but which presents itself primarily as fast moving and fun – a sporty vehicle with a sideline as a general-purpose saloon. This goes on the diagram at TWO.

You can now be more practical than the estate car without buying a pick-up truck. The modern "MPVs" – multi-purpose vehicles – are small comfortable vans with windows and removable car seats in the back: utility with general-purpose influence at SEVEN.

And down at the foot of the diagram, we have not the practical "moderated" pragmatism of the family saloon, but the attempt to marry sporty and utility without compromising either. The modern "SUV" or "sports utility vehicle" is a solidly built, box-shaped four-wheel drive – with a stylish finish and a powerful sporty engine. The larger more functional SUVs belong at FIVE, the smaller sportier ones at FOUR.

Some observations from the analysis.

The vertical scale is a scale of engine size: sporty and utility both demand more power.

There is a THREE-SIX-NINE "triangle of simplicity": the mass market general purpose family saloon at NINE; and the uncompromising simplicity of both the two-seater sports car at THREE and the pick-up truck at SIX. Those who buy at these points are focused on a single priority as they make their choice. The next vehicle on their wish list is likely to be one of the other three vehicles on the THREE-SIX-NINE "triangle of simplicity".

The other points – the six points on "the hexagon of complexity" – represent the interaction of the three key elements: sporty, utility, and the moderating influence of "general-purpose" requirements. Purchasers of these vehicles are allowing these three items on their "vehicle wish-list" to interact as they make their purchasing decision – so buyers who have bought on the hexagon before are likely to buy on the hexagon again.

And this is where this "fun analysis" stumbled into a fascinating new area of study: we have started using the language of human choices – and that is the language of the strategy board.

Consider your own next purchase – to supplement or replace your current vehicle. Your gut reaction probably says that it will be another standard low-cost family saloon. But is there something in your head suggesting that something like a pick-up truck would be really useful? And something in your heart that would just love something a bit more sporty, like an open-top two-seater?

The enneagram of retail road vehicles is about human choices: the human choices that create and define this particular market; the human choices made in the three centers of intelligence which are head and heart and gut. And so it would make perfect logical sense if the enneagram of retail road vehicles mapped fairly accurately on to the enneagram of human decision-making – otherwise known as the strategy board. And this is how it might look:

- NINE – keep it simple – the general-purpose family saloon.

- ONE – full of restrained energy – the saloon with the discrete sporty upgrade.

- TWO – full of the dreams and images of the heart but still wanting to be helpful – the flashy five-seater.

- Competitive THREE: the two-seater sports car.

- Individualist FOUR: the stylish compact SUV.

- Observer FIVE: the high and powerful SUV.

- Practical SIX: the pick-up truck.

- Generalist SEVEN: the multi-purpose vehicle.

- And strong, confident, challenging, lumbering EIGHT: the heavyweight version of that family saloon.

And many people do indeed "drive by type" in accordance with this analysis – and if not by type, then by one of the linked types, along one of the paths across the board.

The market for retail road vehicles is defined by human choices. An enneagram analysis of those human choices has revealed a nine-part correlation with the strategy board – and the intriguing possibility that enneagrams of other human endeavors might also correlate with head and heart and gut, and so with the strategy board itself.

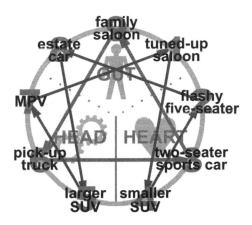

The enneagram of mainstream politics

Mainstream political debate has two competing ideologies: capitalism and socialism, the right and the left. These become the energy points – THREE and SIX – for an enneagram analysis of mainstream politics.

For the most part, contemporary western democracies operate in a pragmatic "center ground" of politics, wholly committed to neither ideology but operating a "mixed economy": a free market and self-reliance in some areas, state control and state provision in others. This "moderated" center ground becomes point NINE in the analysis.

Those who tend to favor the free market and self-reliance are conventionally called "right wing," and those who favor state control and state provision are conventionally called "left wing."

The full spectrum of the debate can now be arranged around the diagram.

Each country will have to do its own analysis of individuals and parties – but for the UK, New Labour has been the epitome of NINE politics: a pragmatic government of the center ground.

It operates on the THREE-SIX-NINE "triangle of simplicity." It can talk in the language of both capitalism and socialism, praising both the freedom of choice and self-reliance implicit in the free market, and the sense of community, interdependence, and common action implicit in universal provision.

It accommodates – sometimes with some tension – its two wings: the center left of the mainstream union movement at ONE, and the center right at EIGHT, which feels quite at home with New Labour's continuing program of "part-privatizations" and increasing private sector involvement at all levels of government.

The Conservative Party and the Liberal Democrats have taken up residence at SEVEN and TWO respectively – two of the only spaces left on the diagram with New Labour proving so versatile from its base at NINE.

It was all very different in the 1980s. In 1984 and 1985, the battle of the ideologies in the UK was fought out in the streets – literally at times – between the miners under Arthur Scargill and the right wing government of Margaret Thatcher.

In retrospect – and looking at this enneagram analysis – the issues were fairly moderate, but very clearly of the left and of the right. Scargill wanted state subsidies for a major core industry – still a fairly common approach for many governments throughout the western world. Thatcher wanted the provision of a basic, readily available, global commodity to operate on free market principles – also a fairly common approach throughout the world. In terms of the enneagram of political debate, this is just a ONE-EIGHT spat – but the stakes were very high in terms of jobs and therefore the economies of several large regions.

What each of the main players did to raise the temperature so much – apart from refusing to find common ground – was to go to the extreme under pressure, following the links to the bottom of the diagram. Scargill began to talk the language of communist revolution, and Thatcher won few friends when she referred to the mineworkers as "the enemy within."

The 1980s was also the decade of the SDP – emerging from one party, forming an alliance with another, and surviving briefly as a splinter group when the alliance partners merged. There were brave political journeys for many of those involved. Some moderate Tories found that a decade had taken them all the way from EIGHT to TWO. David Owen seemed to start at ONE and end up at SEVEN. If UK political debate since 1997 has been conducted on New Labour's triangle of simplicity, political debate in the 1980s was conducted on the hexagon of complexity.

It has often been said that socialism is the politics of the heart while capitalism is the politics of the head. Socialism dreams of how the world could be or should be given that we are all human beings "with a heart": it is the politics of emotions and visions and dreams, of reaching out to the world. Capitalism looks at how the world works, assumes that that is essentially how it is going to be, and works from there: it is the politics of observation, logic, analysis, and planning.

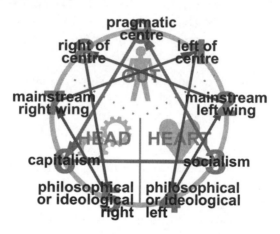

Socialism is the politics of the heart zone – at TWO and THREE and FOUR. At its practical TWO it longs to care for every one of its people like a big mother, "from the cradle to the grave." At its central THREE it tries to inspire everyone to pull together as a team to achieve great things. At its philosophical or ideological FOUR it longs to create a beautiful world. And socialism's opponents call it "the nanny state" at TWO, and "the politics of envy" at FOUR, and accuse it of deceit in its efforts to present a leading, achieving image at THREE. Socialism's proponents and opponents are both right. Corrupted – managed and populated by corrupted humankind – socialism does indeed become the politics of the heart zone's temptations: a smothering nanny-ism and envy and deceit, plus anger at ONE. Redeemed – promoted by good people – it becomes the politics of the heart zone's gifts: compassion and beauty and inspiration, plus fairness for all at ONE.

Capitalism is the politics of the head zone – at SEVEN and SIX and FIVE. At its practical SEVEN it sets people free to try out countless new ideas and inventions and businesses and schemes, each pursuing their own route to their own chosen happiness, rejoicing in this very freedom as a good in itself, hoping that everything will work out well for everyone: SEVEN the optimist-generalist with the gift of joy. At its central SIX it likes to stick with what it knows and honor and reward all that is or has been good: it has a certain loyalty and faithfulness built into the way it works. At its philosophical or ideological FIVE it observes the world with a certain detached objectivity and speaks about it with objective wisdom. And capitalism's opponents call it "the politics of greed" at FIVE, and conservative to the point of cowardice at SIX, and use "consumerism" as a synonym for self-centered, self-defeating gluttony at SEVEN. Capitalism's proponents and opponents are both right. Corrupted – managed and populated by corrupted humankind – capitalism does indeed become the politics of the head zone's temptations: greed and gluttony and fear, plus arrogance at EIGHT. Redeemed – promoted by good people – it becomes the politics of the head zone's gifts: joyful diversity, faithfulness, even wisdom – and a keen sense of justice at EIGHT.

In passing we could note that the center ground of politics often has the gut zone's benefits – it can be just and peaceable and patient. And the center ground's politicians sometimes submit to the gut zone's temptations: idleness perhaps, and in political debate, a little too much political arrogance and anger. Justice and patience and peace would not be bad goals for the modern center ground of politics. And down at the foot of the diagram: utterly corrupted ideologically driven governments of left and right have looked remarkably similar to each other in their oppression of their peoples; and in contrast there is no more refreshingly honest political conversation than that between retired grandees of left and right who are no longer cursed by detailed policy making or the need for re-election, discussing their shared sacred ideology that all are born equal in dignity and value, and the only mystery and disagreement is how to turn that ideology into a practical policy. In corrupt form or redeemed form, left and right find that they do indeed meet at the extremes.

If we dare to talk names, the analysis can be developed to include individuals – for example, there is indeed a lot of the NINE about Tony Blair. He likes to keep his politics simple, and will not bother having an opinion about something unless it has practical applicable value in the here and now. NINE's security type is THREE: the 1997 election campaign involved creating a sense that the entire nation was pulling together as a team to create a new beginning full of new hope – all very THREE – and in the wake of 11 September 2001, he presented the Labour Party Conference with a vision whereby all decent people everywhere in the world would pull together to save the world, one continent at a time. The stress type would be SIX: under pressure, Blair is surprisingly quick to call in the private sector to try to sort things out. And when clinging to false security back at THREE: the biggest complaint against New Labour is that "spin" sometimes seems to stretch all the way to "deceit," the temptation of THREE.

Gordon Brown is a good example of someone operating politically at one of their link types. As the dour Scot whose guiding principle is prudence, he has the nature of SIX, but his politics – don't tell Blair – are all discreetly THREE. While nobody is looking, he keeps piling up new benefits and tax breaks for the poor, and especially for those – a hint of SIX – who take low-paid work rather than no work at all. He remains pragmatic about all of this, placing him confidently on the THREE-SIX-NINE triangle, and therefore in tune with the New Labour "project." The widely rumored "sparky" relationship with Blair is the classic form of relationship for people at the opposite ends – personally or politically – of an internal arrow on the diagram.

Margaret Thatcher was a classic EIGHT. Determined and unstoppable, she really would have stand-up arguments across the cabinet table, and respect people for taking a stand: the rest she dismissed as "wets." With the miners she pushed it right to the limit – and won in the end – but eventually the country had had enough. In retrospect, while she led the way in many areas, her main policies while in power are now seen as very much in the mainstream, only just right of center – even if she had extremist moments, visiting the foot of the diagram. Her campaign for the renewal of the inner cities even took her over to security type TWO for a while, and she put the interventionist Michael Heseltine in charge.

Scargill in contrast was a classic ONE. There was a moralistic perfectionism about his stance and he spluttered with indignation if challenged. His energy was limitless, and there was no room for an inch of compromise. Apart from his occasional trips to the foot of the diagram, most of his policies are surprisingly moderate. The main tax policy of his own Socialist Labour Party today is to double the personal allowance for income tax – which sounds quite radical until you do the sums, and compare it to what Gordon Brown already has in hand.

And so it appears to be the case that many people do indeed do politics "by type," mapping the enneagram of politics on to the strategy board. The option to follow a link or use a wing means that nobody's politics are fixed or predetermined: a SIXish chancellor can be politically all NINE and THREE; the strategy board's FOURs and FIVEs have easy links into the mainstream of politics in the top half of the diagram or to the other side on a wing; and SEVENs and EIGHTs and ONEs and TWOs can all take fairly confident trips across the board.

And the logic of it all is this: that an enneagram analysis of any human endeavor or choice is likely to map on to the strategy board whenever there are two contrasting approaches – for head and for heart – and a third neutral or moderating place, for the gut reaction.

The enneagram of the Trinity

Fundamentally the enneagram is a tool "for examining the properties of certain three-part systems" – so it should be possible to follow its logic and give some consideration to that ultimate "three-part system," the Trinity.

The doctrine of the Trinity is a model for helping to understand God. It is not explained directly in Scripture: it was developed by the church to emphasize the key things we understand, as Christian people, about the one God revealed to us in Jesus Christ.

If there is to be an enneagram of the Trinity, it will be an enneagram of the ways in which human beings understand God and relate to God. The classic "three persons of the Trinity" will provide its shape, and the finished analysis should clarify some of the "properties" of this "three-part system."

To begin, we are looking for one main contrast: not so much a contrast "within God" as a contrast in the ways in which "human beings understand God and relate to God." Ideally it will be a head-heart contrast – and here it is, among the so-called "proofs for the existence of God."

The church still officially recognizes two proofs for the existence of God, which are independent of the story of Jesus – and they can be categorized immediately as one for the head and one for the heart.

The first is the argument from creation: the fact that something exists rather than nothing; indeed, the fact that there is space for the "something" to exist at all.

From this we discern the existence of a creator.

Science is no problem here. Science explains in ever-greater detail how creation works – not how it came to be here in the first place.

This "proof" does not tell us much about the nature of God, but it does show that we are ultimately dependent on something far greater than ourselves – and we can name it both "God" and "creator."

This logical rational proof is a proof "for the head."

The other "proof" is very different – but it also works backward from what we can see to what we cannot see.

The second proof recognizes this: that every human heart is yearning – for meaning, for purpose, for something more than this physical life alone can provide.

This is the proof "for the heart."

Again, it does not tell us much about the nature of God – but what the heart so evidently seeks we can name as "God."

As Christian people, we would also name this God "for the human heart" as "Holy Spirit" – God who will dwell in our hearts.

In the official teaching of the church, these "proofs for the existence of God" are mere sidelines, noted in passing. They are the proofs "independent of the story of Jesus," proofs for those who will never hear of Jesus.

Logic and reason – for the head – have identified God who is creator. The longing of the human heart points to God who is Holy Spirit. Now Jesus of Nazareth is placed at the very center of Christian faith and teaching: God in our human flesh and blood – incarnate and directly engaging with our world.

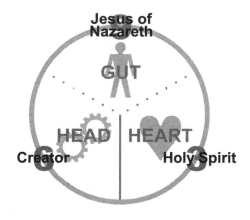

Jesus in his years in human flesh and blood – "Jesus of Nazareth" – is the very center of the system at NINE.

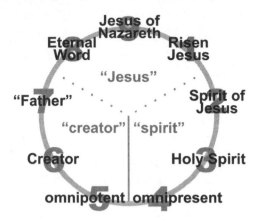

"The Risen Jesus" of the New Testament – after the resurrection – is still Jesus, but has rather more in common with the concept of God that we name Holy Spirit – for this is not only the Jesus of the resurrection appearances, but the Jesus who met Saint Paul on the road to Damascus, after the ascension, and the Jesus who meets with us today in the Eucharist. This Risen Jesus is still Jesus – but distinctively at the "Holy Spirit" end of the "Jesus" zone: at ONE in our enneagram of the trinity.

Saint John's Gospel begins with the wonderful poetic preface naming Jesus as the eternal Word of God – with God even before time began. This is a concept of Jesus close to the creator – at the "creator" end of the "Jesus" zone, at EIGHT.

One of the difficulties in trying to read the trinity straight from the Scriptures is that Saint Paul often uses two phrases almost interchangeably: "Spirit of Jesus" and "Spirit of Holiness" – or Holy Spirit. But this need not be a problem. Saint Paul's "Spirit of Jesus" is a perfectly valid concept of God – beyond "Risen Jesus" and on the way toward "Holy Spirit": it belongs at the "Jesus" end of the "Holy Spirit" zone.

At the foot of the diagram we expect "creator" and "Holy Spirit" to meet at the extremes in a way that is distinct from their interaction at the top of the diagram. Here we see beyond God as creator to God as omnipotent – infinitely powerful. And we see beyond God as "Holy Spirit with us" to God as "Holy Spirit everywhere" – omnipresent.

And finally, at the "Jesus" end of the "creator" zone, we can place the name that Jesus invites us to use for our creator God. The one who made us is involved in our lives, and cares for us like a perfect parent: Jesus invites us to call on God as "Father," a human image for our creator God – at the "Jesus" end of the "creator" zone.

The classic model of God as Trinity has been expanded through the enneagram into a model of nine "concepts" of the one God – drawing in more scriptural images, allowing the three concepts to blend more naturally into one, and retaining all the distinctiveness of the classic trinitarian model.

In the "Jesus" zone we have not only Jesus of Nazareth – God in human flesh in the holy land in AD 30 – but also those other concepts of God the Son: the eternal Word and the Risen Jesus.

In the "spirit" zone we have the God who is the true "Spirit of Jesus" – not only in our hearts, but everywhere in creation.

In the "creator" zone we have the omnipotent God who is also the creator God – and who cares for us and watches over us, the "Father" God.

At the top of the vertical scale we have Jesus of Nazareth – vulnerable even to death, walking the earth at a particular time in a particular place. At the foot of the diagram we see the God who is eternal, all-powerful, and everywhere. Those who talk less of the Trinity and more of "God and Jesus" have the two ends of this scale in mind. This is also the Great Creator Spirit of eastern Orthodox prayer.

Moving up the vertical scale, THREE and SIX present the God who creates, and longs to be in our hearts – more intimate concepts than those at FIVE and FOUR – and then SEVEN and TWO and EIGHT and ONE are concepts of God ever more closely connected with the concept of God made present in Christ.

The final part of the analysis would involve the connections made by the arrows – and any correspondence with the strategy board. And it appears that many Christian people do indeed relate to God primarily through home base and its two connected types.

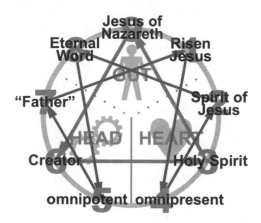

For SIXes, God is our creator and we are God's team – called by Jesus of Nazareth and equipped by the Holy Spirit in our hearts: SIX and NINE and THREE.

For NINEs, Jesus of Nazareth is our example, our leader, and our guide, uniting and bringing peace – connecting us to God the creator, and sending the Holy Spirit: NINE and SIX and THREE.

For THREEs, the Holy Spirit is with us, inspiring us, and leading us, making all things possible – uniting us with Jesus of Nazareth and with our creator: THREE and NINE and SIX.

For ONEs, the perfection of the Risen Jesus is central – opening the way to God who is the compassionate Father and to God who is omnipresent Spirit: ONE and SEVEN and FOUR.

For EIGHTs, the sense of God's eternal Word confronting the world is central – at EIGHT – and the contrast within the nature of God is God's omnipotence at FIVE alongside God's compassion – the Spirit of Jesus – at TWO.

For TWOs, the Spirit of Jesus in our hearts is central. This Spirit is everywhere – accessible to every human heart – but also confronts the world as the eternal Word: TWO and FOUR and EIGHT.

For SEVENs, God is the Father who will take care of everything – so all will be well, come what may. And the Father God is also the omnipotent God, who was able to bring Jesus even through the ultimate pain of crucifixion and death into resurrection life: SEVEN and FIVE and ONE.

For FOURs, God's Spirit is everywhere – and is the Spirit of Jesus who is risen and alive: FOUR and TWO and ONE.

And for FIVEs, observing the universe, God is the all-powerful one – and yet God longs to relate to us as "Father," and reaches out as the eternal Word: FIVE and SEVEN and EIGHT.

Our enneagram of the Trinity – an analysis of nine aspects or images of God – has mapped on to the strategy board, showing how God reaches out not only to every one of us, but to every part of who we are.

The static enneagram – review

In each of our static enneagram analyses, the method has been the same:

- identify the contrasting concepts – for the left and right zones of the diagram
- identify the neutral or distinctive territory – for the top, central zone
- at the foot of the diagram, identify how the two original concepts "meet at the extremes"
- fill in the remaining points on the diagram.

The analysis then reveals some or all of the following:

- new perspectives on the original left-right contrast
- a meaningful vertical scale
- a meaningful "triangle of simplicity" linking the three main concepts
- a meaningful pattern of more complex connections on the hexagon
- and finally a correspondence with the strategy board – whenever the system is about a human endeavor which correlates with head and heart and gut.

This is the process of analysis that produced the strategy board itself from the three initial concepts of head and heart and gut – and it continues to reveal correlations with the strategy board whenever the contrasting concepts for analysis correspond with these three.

The cyclical enneagram

The cyclical enneagram analyzes cyclical processes – processes that repeat through time. It illustrates and clarifies the concepts contained in words and phrases like "key moment," "point of no return," "back a stage," and "forward planning": once again, the enneagram becomes "a picture worth a thousand words."

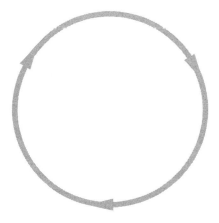

The process itself is represented by clockwise movement around the outer circle of the diagram. This sense of a clockwise progression around the outer circle is the key feature differentiating the cyclical enneagram from the static enneagram.

The analysis of a cyclical process begins with the identification of the "steady state" – the central or neutral or resting state, which represents the beginning and end of each cycle. This is represented by the point at the top of the diagram – point NINE.

The first key moment to identify within the cycle itself is "the point of no return" – the moment when the option to retreat disappears, and the only way to return to the steady state is to complete the cycle.

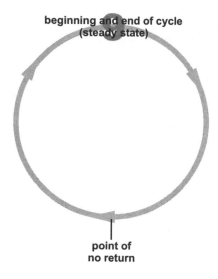

"The point of no return" goes at the foot of the diagram, in the center – diametrically opposite the beginning and ending point.

We now have a sense of an "outward" journey, away from the steady state toward "the point of no return," and a "homeward" journey, by a different route, back from "the point of no return" to the steady state.

The next part of the analysis is the identification of the two "energy points" in the cycle – the two key moments or energies in the cycle that dictate its sense of direction and purpose. These become points THREE and SIX.

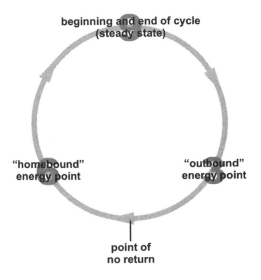

Energy point THREE represents the energy that gives the cycle momentum – taking it out of the steady state toward "the point of no return." It represents "outward bound," "risk taking" energy.

Energy point SIX represents the energy that carries the cycle safely back from "the point of no return" to the steady state: "homeward bound" energy.

Points THREE and SIX and NINE now define the nature of the cycle as a whole. In particular, each dominates its own "phase" – its own third – of the cycle.

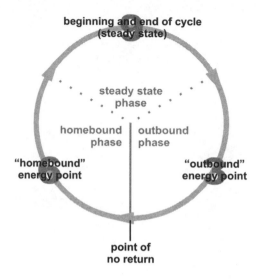

Sometimes it is easier to identify the two energy phases or energy points first, and then identify "the point of no return" which lies between them.

The point of no return is the point at which "the balance is tipped" to move from the outbound phase into the homebound phase. It is the high-energy, high-risk point in the middle of the cycle – quite the opposite of the steady state.

Detail is now added by identifying intermediate stages in the cycle – six altogether: one at the beginning and one at the end of each phase.

ONE and TWO are intermediate stages beginning the cycle, on the way toward the main outbound energy point THREE.

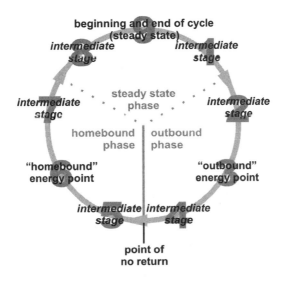

FOUR and FIVE are intermediate stages in the high-energy section of the cycle, immediately before and immediately after the point of no return.

SEVEN and EIGHT are intermediate stages concluding the cycle – on the way back toward NINE from homebound energy point SIX.

The arrows that make up the THREE-SIX-NINE triangle now represent the concept of "going back a stage."

The arrow back from THREE to NINE represents a retreat: deciding against completion of the cycle before "the point of no return" is passed.

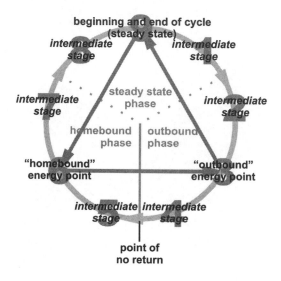

The arrow back from NINE to SIX represents a repeat of the last part – only – of the most recent cycle, rather than a whole new cycle.

And the arrow back from SIX to THREE represents a high risk, high energy repeat of the most intensive part of the cycle, without first returning to the steady state phase.

The hexagon represents a series of more complex "alternative moves" within the cycle.

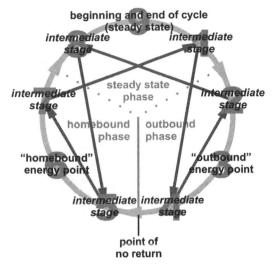

On the right hand side of the diagram, before the point of no return, it gives the option of a confident leap forward, almost as soon as the cycle has begun at ONE, all the way out almost to the point of no return, at FOUR. It also suggests – just before the point of no return – the option of a short retreat, back from FOUR to TWO, spending more time in this energy phase before passing "the point of no return."

On the left hand side of the diagram, the extra links suggest a small jump forward from FIVE to SEVEN, and the option to repeat this entire phase with the loop back from EIGHT to FIVE.

Across the top of the diagram, a jump is suggested directly from the end of the homebound energy phase – at SEVEN – right into the beginning of the next cycle, at ONE; and at TWO there is the option to postpone the present cycle in order to tidy up the end of the last one by going back from TWO to EIGHT.

In total there are six "alternative moves" on the hexagon – three forward and three backward, at various stages in the cycle – but their relationship with "the point of no return" is unique. They allow no way of avoiding it going forwards, and they offer no way back once it has been passed.

Even the THREE-SIX-NINE triangle offers no way of avoiding "the point of no return" going forward – although the "back a stage" principle of the triangle does allow a loop back from SIX to THREE, to run the entire "high energy" part of the cycle again.

Some practical examples of cyclical processes will show all of these features in action.

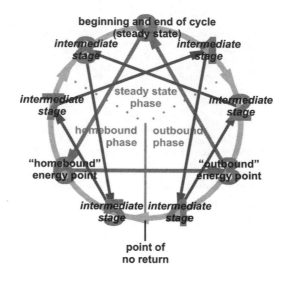

The enneagram of the agricultural year

The agricultural year is a cyclical process – through the seasons of the year: "the seed time and the harvest," with winter – the fallow time – in between.

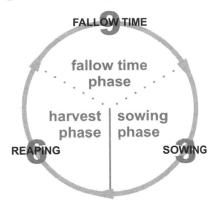

Immediately, the steady state phase and the two energy points have been identified: fallow time, sowing, and reaping – as NINE and THREE and SIX.

On the way toward that first definitive moment – the actual sowing of the seed at THREE – stage ONE might be the preparation of the seed for sowing, toward the end of the fallow time, and stage TWO might be the plowing of the field in preparation for the seed.

After the sowing at THREE, stage FOUR might be the initial nurture of the seedlings, and stage FIVE their later nurture to maturity. In between comes the point of no return, at which the decision is made, either seedling by seedling or field by field, that a plant is healthy enough to be worth the investment of nurturing to maturity. Once that decision is made, there is no going back.

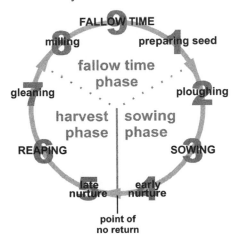

In the fullness of time there is the harvest at SIX. Stage SEVEN might be the gleaning and the tidying of the field, and the securing of by-products like straw from wheat. Stage EIGHT could be the milling of wheat and the laying up of stores for the winter – and at point NINE there is rest and the cycle of the year is complete.

This is the cycle in its natural progression – but other factors can intervene, and these are represented by the internal arrows in the diagram.

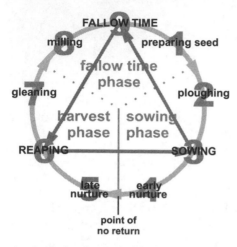

If the "fallow time" of NINE becomes a time of famine, you have to go backward from NINE to SIX to reap where you have not sown – by digging up roots or collecting wild resources to survive.

If birds or mildew destroy the newly sown seed, you have to go back from THREE to NINE to begin preparations all over again.

And if the harvest fails at SIX there is no fallow time – but an immediate return to work at THREE.

On the right hand side of the diagram, before the point of no return – a mature orchard needs some annual early season attention equivalent to the preparation of the seed at ONE, but no plowing or sowing: this could be represented by the arrow from ONE to FOUR, bypassing TWO and THREE.

A decision at early nurture stage FOUR that a plant or a field of plants is too weak to be worth further investment of energy is represented by the arrow from stage FOUR back to stage TWO – two steps back "to have another try" before passing the point of no return.

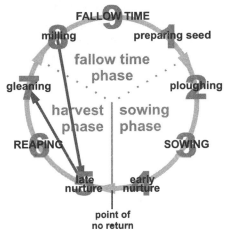

On the left hand side of the diagram, after the point of no return, some crops – like the orchard again – may have a long season, with no specific moment of harvest – bypassing any single point SIX.

Different crops and different fields reaching maturity at different times in the harvest season may create a repeating harvest-season cycle of late nurture, harvesting, gleaning, processing, and more late nurture – all illustrated by the loop back from EIGHT to FIVE – although eventually this "local" cycle ends and the year moves on to fallow time NINE.

And finally, various alternative connections are possible among the intermediate stages that border the fallow period. Across the fallow time, tasks concluding the current season may interact with preparations for the next: part of the harvest may be prepared now for use as next season's seed, making the link forward from SEVEN to ONE; and even as

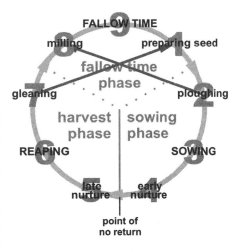

preparations for the new season begin, it may be necessary to return to tasks relating to the end of the previous season, like milling grain and baking bread – the loop back from TWO to EIGHT.

The agricultural year is a regular cyclical process, which might be interrupted or adapted on occasions in a variety of ways, and for a variety of reasons: the nine internal lines of the enneagram illustrate all of the major options.

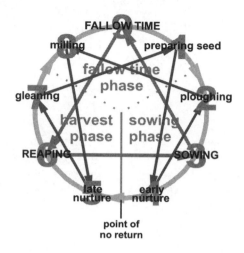

The enneagram of reflection and action

There is a cyclical process called the hermeneutic cycle: the process of reading the Scriptures in one context, applying them to life in a way that changes the context, and then returning to the Scriptures to read them again in the new context – a cycle of "reflection and action."

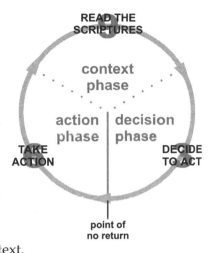

In the cycle of reflection and action, the beginning and end of each cycle – point NINE – is being in a particular context and reading the Scriptures in that context.

The two key moments in the cycle – points THREE and SIX – are the decision to act, and taking the action.

The earliest intermediate stages of the cycle, between reading the Scriptures and deciding to act, are extracting ideals from what is read – stage ONE – and applying those ideals to the context – stage TWO. It then becomes possible to take the decision to act at point THREE.

Having made the decision to take some kind of action, it becomes necessary to formulate a vision of what is possible in practice – what can actually be done in this context to express the ideal on which the decision was based. This is stage FOUR: formulating a detailed vision or plan.

The decision has been made and a plan has been formulated: now we pass the point of no return as we set the plan in motion – stage FIVE.

Point SIX is the center of the action phase. Stage SEVEN is the immediate aftermath, tying up any loose ends, properly completing the task. Stage EIGHT is "debriefing" – initial reflection on the action, and on how the context has now changed. Point NINE is back to the Bible – being in a particular context and reading the Scriptures in that context – "a newspaper in one hand and a Bible in the other" – and so the cycle begins over again.

Any organization or community that seeks to engage with its context in a meaningful and effective way will need to engage in this kind of cycle of reflection and action. If it is to remain relevant in the long term, it needs to engage in the entire cycle repeatedly over time as both the context and the community change.

With the static enneagram, we established that there is often a correspondence between the nine points of the enneagram analysis and the nine sectors of the strategy board – whenever the original left-right contrast correlates with the concepts of head and heart.

The same is found to be true with this enneagram analysis of the cycle of reflection and action.

The decision phase is all about the energy of the heart: choosing to "get involved," motivating the team, and dreaming of what could be. This phase is about getting the decision made and pushing on to the point of no return.

And then, with the decision made and agreed, the action phase is the phase for following the plan through – logically and almost mechanically – if it is to succeed. This is where some objective head energy is required to keep everything on track and to focus on the completion of the plan.

And finally, the context phase is all about engaging directly with the world as it is. It is about an immediate, practical, and direct perception of the situation – perhaps at an almost instinctive and intuitive level: all the essential features of the gut zone.

And so, in a community that is working well, it may well be the NINEs who will peacefully read the Scriptures, compare the world around, and calmly point out the mismatch – speaking hard truths calmly.

Idealistic ONEs would extract the ideals from the Scriptures.

Caring TWOs would apply those ideals to the context – where they already know every hidden need.

Group-leader THREEs would inspire the team to take the decision to act.

Creative FOURs would work out how to give expression to the decision – how to paint it on to the world. They would formulate a vision – a plan – based on the ideals and applicable to the world as it is.

FIVEs are now challenged to apply their wisdom and to use their extensive resources to attend to the fine details and then – when everything is ready – set the plan in motion.

Team member SIXes will faithfully and loyally see the action through.

SEVENs, optimists and generalists and always ready for more, could keep going as others tire – picking up all the loose ends, dealing efficiently with a whole range of small issues in the final stage of the action phase, and staying positive, come what may.

At the debriefing, EIGHTs will be there with a full analysis of everything that has been learned from the experience, as they will have been testing everything out as they went along: the only ones taking careful note – amidst the chaos of battle – of where the real power was hidden, and where the boundaries of possibility may lie.

And once the adventure is done, NINEs will welcome everybody peacefully back home.

It is the clearest possible demonstration of the assertion that everybody has a role – that everybody has a part to play.

In practice, of course, not every community functions this well. The internal arrows in the diagram illustrate some of the ways in which organizations may end up failing to interact successfully with their context – by repeatedly missing out some essential stages, or by becoming stuck in a "local loop," continuously repeating just one small part of the cycle.

On the THREE-SIX-NINE triangle: if an organization fails to maintain proper contact with its environment – its context – it ends up looping back repeatedly along the arrow from SIX to THREE. There is plenty of decision-making and planning and action – but instead of going on to reflect on the changing context, the organization goes straight

back to decision-making again. It is depending on everything being unchanged since the last time it checked – information that could be hopelessly dated. It has ended up "out of touch," ineffective, and irrelevant to "the real world." It needs someone to intervene with a "reality check," shaking the organization out of its local loop with some harsh news from "the real world": someone with some NINE.

An organization that never manages to pull together and make a decision is stuck in the loop described by the arrow from NINE back to SIX. There may be plenty of action, and tidying up afterwards, and debriefing, and rest and reflection, but instead of taking the time to look again at the ideals of the organization, and apply them to the context in a

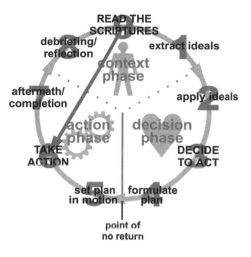

new way, the organization simply falls into a cycle of doing things the way they have always been done. It needs someone with some insight and some inspirational team-building skills to show the organization that there is another way – or a whole range of other ways – for being true to their ideals, and having an impact: someone with some THREE.

And some organizations pass grand resolutions unanimously at well-structured meetings – but never get around to acting on them. The decisions are relevant and visionary – true to the context and the group's ideals but the organization fails to make it into the action phase and loops back repeatedly from THREE to NINE. It needs someone to point

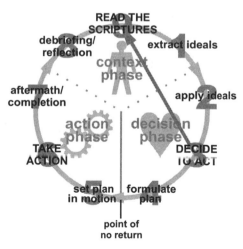

out that decisions are only meaningful if committed action follows: someone with some SIX.

Appendix 1: The enneagram

There are three potential "local loops" on the hexagon of arrows. The arrow back from EIGHT to FIVE can create a loop, which is even more full of action than the loop-back from NINE to SIX – and while it is sometimes useful to repeat an action once or twice, reflection and new decisions – the rest of the cycle – will be appropriate in due course.

The arrow back from FOUR to TWO can hone a decision – but eventually the perfected plan has to be set in motion and carried through, and then there needs to be new reflection on the context – and these are the functions of the rest of the cycle.

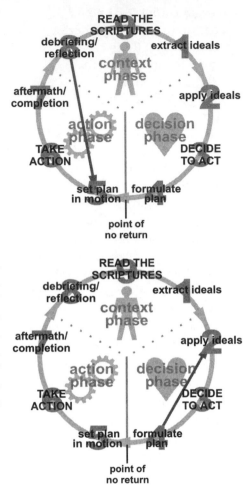

The local loop that remains most in touch with its context is the one defined by the arrow back from TWO to EIGHT: it is the only local loop that includes all three stages of the context phase. I suspect that modern "NINEish" center-ground government operates most of the time in this loop: there is reflection and there are ideals, but before

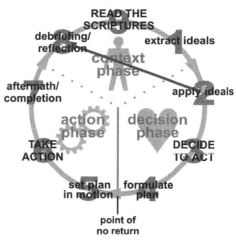

there is a chance for a major new policy to emerge, someone comes in with a report from a focus group or a small trial and the brief inspiration of TWO is pulled straight back to EIGHT. The consequence is that modern center-ground government is often all tinkering rather than genuinely innovative planning or action – although it is probably better for a government in a modern democracy to be "too in touch" with its context than not in touch at all.

And before we leave the arrows, it is worth noting that the three arrows that represent "jumps forward" are not always positive moves. The jump forward from ONE to FOUR is certainly possible – but rushing through the decision phase could mean that the decision is not as good as it could have been, and could leave many people feeling left out – unwilling to join in with the action phase.

The jump forward from FIVE to SEVEN may represent a failure to enter fully into the action that was required.

And the jump forward from SEVEN to ONE could represent too little reflection and too hasty a launch into another cycle of decision and action.

And from this it becomes clear once again that the entire community needs to participate if the community is to engage with its context in a meaningful and effective way. Through the nine stages of the cycle, the "baton of responsibility" is passed from sector to sector – from the people of type NINE, to the people of type ONE, to the people of type TWO and so on – inviting and requiring every member of the community to fulfill their own specific role, their own vocation. The individuals are largely static in their natural home base: it is the life of the effective community as a whole that progresses clockwise through the nine stages of the cycle.

Finally it is worth considering the cycle from the perspective of an individual.

Working alone – rather than in a community – individuals are likely to keep on "playing their strongest hand."

For NINEs that means relying on their clear understanding of the context, rather than complex decision-making or extended long-term planning: in interacting with the world, they will "keep it simple."

ONEs are likely to cling on to extracted ideals – becoming idealists and perfectionists, and being always "on their best behavior."

TWOs will apply the ideals to the situations around them – so in any society where giving and caring are ideals, TWOs will apply those ideals: they will "give and care."

THREEs will focus on making those key decisions that turn ideals into action: they will emerge as leaders, inspirers, and achievers.

FOURs are best at formulating detailed plans based on the ideals. Working alone, the ideals in question will be their own ideals – and they will seek to live life in every detail according to those ideals: their maxim in all things, "be true to yourself,"

FIVEs' strongest hand is tipping the balance that sets the plan into motion. They will give due consideration to the timing as well as the detail. They will always "think it through first."

SIXes are confident and unwavering, working through the action as prescribed in the plan: their strategy when working all alone will be to stick with the plan they know.

SEVENs are best at dealing with all the loose ends. As individuals meeting the world they will deal with whatever appears, and move on – and "stay positive come what may."

And EIGHTs are best at making sense of whatever has happened: working alone, hungry for the information to interpret and assess, they will need to make things happen in order to asses them: they will always be "testing people out."

The cycle of reflection and action – like the strategy board – is all about human choices for interaction with the world around. We are mapping the same basic themes – and the features on the two maps coincide once again.

The enneagram of the church year

The church year is an annual cycle of festivals and commemorations – and once again an enneagram analysis helps to illustrate and emphasize the nature, and the value, of the cycle.

It is the significance rather than the length of each season, which holds the key to this analysis – as reflected in the amount of Scripture and significant theology attached to each season. Taking this approach, the events of Holy Week take up a significant proportion of the cycle.

Once again we find a correspondence – not only with the strategy board, but also with the cycle of reflection and action.

Advent is both the expectant beginning and the triumphant end of the cycle of the year. In Advent we recall the anticipation of the people of the Old Covenant – looking forward to the coming of the Messiah – and we also look forward to the return of Christ in glory at the end of time. For the people of the Old Covenant and for ourselves it is the season of waiting in trust and peace for God

to come to us, in God's perfect time: it is the resting state of the cycle, the beginning and end point NINE.

The key moment of action being taken – of work being done – is the death of Christ on the cross, in which Jesus is faithful and loyal to the end. It is the action point – and it is the sector for faithfulness and loyalty – at SIX.

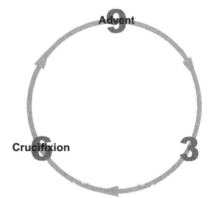

In the sequence of events that leads to the cross, the point of no return is the arrest in the garden of Gethsemane. This comes between the Last Supper – which we have already seen has the nature of FOUR – and the process of the trial – during which Jesus remains silent, observing, wiser than any merely human soul, and quite detached from the humiliation being inflicted upon him. The process of the trial belongs at FIVE.

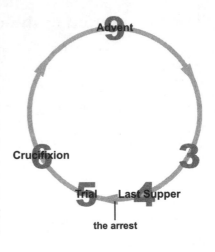

The work of the cross culminates in resurrection – point SEVEN: a great and profound and eternal joy, defeating all – literally all – the pain of the world.

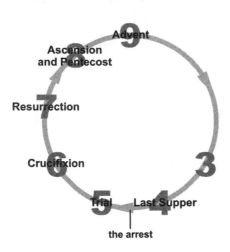

Forty days later, Jesus' final "debriefing" of the disciples concludes with the ascension, at EIGHT, when Jesus ascends to the right hand of God – to the place of kingdom and power and glory for ever. And then to empower the church for the time that lies ahead, the Spirit comes at Pentecost – pushing the boundaries of the possible – to continue and complete the work of Christ in the world.

And in the wake of that first Pentecost, with great anticipation we look again for the coming of Christ – all around us now in a thousand different ways, and in great glory at the end of time: the contemporary Advent, the "now," point NINE.

Energy point THREE has to be the moment of decision – when Jesus determined to go through with the challenge that was created by the compassionate will of God and the sinfulness of the world. That moment of decision is represented by the very beginning of Jesus' earthly ministry: his public baptism by John, and the overcoming of the temptations in the wilderness. From that time onwards, the pattern is set. These particular events have Jesus setting an example in baptism for others to follow, and then, in the wilderness temptations, working out his model of true leadership and "achievement" for the years ahead – and this is THREE. In the church year, it is Lent.

The seasons between Advent and Lent are Christmas and the Epiphany. Christmas is all about the wonderful ideal of the divine and the human uniting in the very birth – the very concept – of Christ, the perfect human being, the one who is pure and who will purify the world for God. Celebrating the perfect, the ideal – Christmas has the

nature of ONE. It moves us out of the "waiting" of Advent into the life of Christ – and the cycle of the year.

The feast of the Epiphany is kept twelve days later – the traditional date for the arrival of the Magi. In the Epiphany, we see the first application of the ideals that are to be made known in

293

Christ: we see God in Christ welcoming the Gentiles. And Epiphany is also about adoration and gifts for this child: Epiphany is TWO.

All down the right hand side of the diagram we see the events that lead inevitably toward "the point of no return." And from that point onwards, we see the process by which the work of Christ is completed – and established "until the end of the age."

The internal arrows within the diagram now make valuable connections as we meditate on these nine great themes of our salvation.

In Advent, at NINE, as we await the coming glory of our salvation, it is worth reflecting on the cost – at the cross, at SIX. Kneeling at the foot of the cross on Good Friday, at SIX, we are taken back to the reflective mode of Lent, at THREE. In Lent, at THREE, as we ponder the cost of our salvation, we can continue in the sure knowledge that our salvation is nevertheless at hand – the sure hope of Advent at NINE.

At Christmas, at ONE, we reflect on the incarnation, and where it leads – the Last Supper at FOUR, the breaking of bread. Whenever bread is broken at FOUR, we can offer our adoration to the living Christ, like the Magi who recognized the Christ at TWO – recognizing Jesus, like the early disciples, in the breaking of bread (Luke 24:30-31). Adoring the Christ child at Epiphany, at TWO, we are struck by the fact that this child is also lord of all, at the right hand of God the creator – this child is the ascended Christ of EIGHT, and present with us today through the gift of Pentecost, also at EIGHT.

The cost of Christ's glory at EIGHT was the earthly humiliation of the trial at FIVE (Philippians 2:6-11). Each Good Friday, hearing again the account of that trial at FIVE, we have the privilege of knowing that the day of resurrection is coming, at SEVEN. And on the day of resurrection, at SEVEN, Christ is once again among us, and we rejoice again with the joy of Christ's birth among us at ONE.

God in Christ began and completed this cycle once only as the historic Jesus of Nazareth – beginning and ending at the right hand of God with humankind waiting in hope and anticipation. It is to remind us of these key events – the foundations of our Christian lives – that the church recalls them all in sequence year by year.

The enneagram of the Lord's Prayer

At the very conclusion of the main text, the Lord's Prayer stood as an intriguing single example of a cyclical enneagram – complete with a sense of clockwise motion and a line-by-line correlation with the nine types of the strategy board.

Having now examined the full theory of the cyclical enneagram, it is time to revisit the Lord's Prayer.

Let us begin not with the prayer but with the more general teaching of Jesus. There are three truly radical aspects of Jesus' teaching, identified in these three words: Father, kingdom, and forgiveness.

Jesus taught that God is "Abba, Father" – a radically new perspective on the nature of God and the relationship between fallen humankind and its creator. It is the tenderness and intimacy of that name – "Abba" – which makes this teaching unique.

Jesus proclaimed the kingdom: the kingdom of heaven or the kingdom of God, growing like a mustard seed, leavening the dough, already among us and yet still to come. It presents a unique and radical vision for the future of redeemed humankind – a future already begun.

And the action that makes this kingdom possible is the third radical theme in the teaching of Jesus: forgiveness. Jesus teaches that God forgives us – again and again – and that we must forgive one another – again and again.

We can now arrange these three themes according to the cycle of reflection and action.

The radical new discovery about our context is this: that God is "Abba, Father." Of the three "radical teachings," this is the teaching at point NINE.

In this new context, humankind is invited to participate in the kingdom of God. This teaching becomes the first energy point of the cycle: we are invited to choose for the kingdom, to grasp the vision of what could be.

The third teaching – forgiveness – naturally becomes the energy point in the action phase of the cycle. It is the action that God takes to make all of this possible. It is the action that we are invited to take, to make the beginnings of the kingdom possible on earth for ourselves and for those around us.

And the three teachings form a cycle, because it is the action of forgiveness which reconciles us with God, and allows us to approach God in the first place with those intimate words, "Our Father."

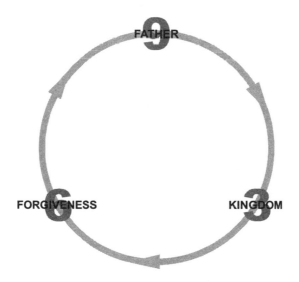

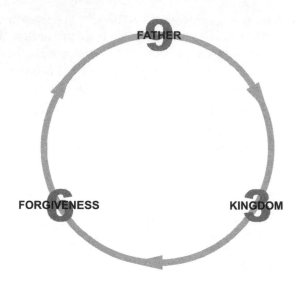

These three key points form the basis of our prayer: beginning and ending in God with "Our Father" and "Amen"; praying for the coming of the kingdom with "thy kingdom come"; and acknowledging the central role of forgiveness, from God to us and from us to those around us – "forgive us our trespasses, as we forgive those who trespass against us." These three lines and the "Amen" form the central framework of the prayer.

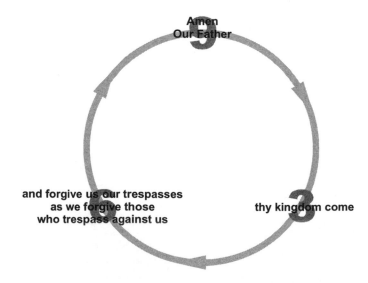

And now we add the intermediate stages: from the understanding of the context at NINE, we extract the ideals at ONE, with images of God's heaven. The beginning of the decision phase is the practical application of ourselves to those ideals by entering into relationship with God who is our Father: the acknowledgment that is also worship, "hallowed be thy name."

After deciding for the kingdom, we turn the principle into a more detailed plan: "thy will be done on earth, as it is in heaven," intending to "paint the beauty of heaven onto the rough canvas of this world."

The point of no return is passed and we contemplate the practicalities of bringing heaven to earth – beginning with supplies: daily bread at FIVE. The main practical matter is forgiveness at SIX. Some of the other items – picked up at SEVEN – are "deliverance from" temptation and evil and pain. And as the kingdom begins to emerge on earth as promised, God is acknowledged as the one who makes it possible and who energizes every part of the cycle: "for thine is the kingdom, the power, and the glory, now and for ever."

"Amen."

The cycle of this prayer takes us through the whole process of recognizing "in our guts" the nature of God, choosing "in our hearts" for God and God's kingdom, committing "with our heads" to the practical action required, and then recognizing "in our guts" once again that the whole process belongs to God.

To repeat the cycle is to deepen its impact upon us and within us. It is no accident that the prayer delivers us at the end back to "our guts" where it began. It is no coincidence that for centuries the prayer has been used repetitively – repeated over and over – as cycle upon cycle it offers up all that we are to God again and again, and binds us into Jesus' radical project: "Father, kingdom, forgiveness, Father, kingdom, forgiveness..."

We recognized in the main text the importance of each line of the prayer to the people of that "home base" in particular: their need for that line, and their offering of that line. The lines of the prayer connected by arrows are also going to be naturally important to the people of each type. And the lines opposite the home base may present a particular challenge: it is all within the essential logic of the strategy board and the enneagram.

We are called to play our part in the community that offers this prayer. We are also called to pray the whole of this prayer with the whole of who we are: head and heart and gut; one whole humanity, one whole prayer.

Cyclical enneagram – review

In each of our cyclical enneagram analyses, we have followed the same method:

- identify the point which represents the beginning and end of each cycle

- identify the "outbound" energy, the "homebound" energy, and the point of no return

- identify the various intermediate stages in the cycle.

The analysis then reveals some or all of the following:

- the contrast between the outbound and the homebound phases of the cycle

- the "high energy" nature of passing the point of no return

- alternative moves in the cycle – for better or for worse – along the nine internal arrows

- and finally a correspondence with the strategy board – whenever the cycle is defined by human choices and therefore by head and heart and gut.

The enneagram has proved to be a powerful tool for examining the properties of various systems. The strategy board itself is just one extended example of an enneagram analysis – making full use of the great potential of this powerful logical analytical tool.

Appendix 2

From the Enneagram
to the Strategy Board

Introduction

The enneagram is generally presented as a system of three parts:

- a list of nine types of people, variously described
- their arrangement in a circle in a specific order
- their further interconnection by a distinctive irregular pattern of internal arrows.

Over a hundred books have been published on this material in the last twenty years. It has been presented variously as a tool for personal growth, a program for business management, and a resource for spiritual direction.

In all of this, each part of the system has been endlessly described – but never explained.

In the gap where the explanation should be, all kinds of popular myths have flourished. The most widespread is the idea that the enneagram was passed down as secret knowledge among eastern sages before being brought to the west by a handful of privileged teachers – a myth which can be endlessly embroidered, to the delight of some and the consternation of others.

Scratch the surface of this myth and it simply disappears. There is no evidence for the enneagram's distinctive diagram existing in any source or tradition earlier than the twentieth century. The only correlation with its list of nine types of people before the twentieth century is in the soundly Christian work of the desert fathers on "the theology of the passions" – the origin of our contemporary list of "seven deadly sins."

Into "the gap where the explanation should be" comes the present text.

From first principles – from the first page – it explains as it describes.

This appendix describes the "real" history of the enneagram – and then its development, from the enneagram to the Strategy Board.

The diagram

The distinctive diagram that is the enneagram first appears in the work of George Gurdjieff in the early twentieth century.

Gurdjieff's followers Ouspensky, Bennett, and Blake describe "the enneagram of process" – and reject the later work linking the diagram with nine "types" of people. There are, however, two intriguing links with the later work: Gurdjieff identified three "brains" or "centers of function" similar to head and heart and gut – the intellectual, the emotional, and the instinctual; and Bennett is credited with having arranged the lines of the Lord's Prayer around the diagram.

For the purists, "the enneagram of personality types" remains just one of many enneagrams – just one of many uses of the diagram. The difficult part is tracking down those "other uses": no writer on "the enneagram of personality types" discusses them – and the work of Gurdjieff and his followers is almost impenetrably obscure. But in the midst of this obscurity there are clues – especially the idea of clockwise motion representing a "process" round the outer circle, with NINE as the starting and ending point and THREE and SIX as "shock points" or "energy points."

The rest – Appendix 1 above – is entirely new work by the present author, asking the question "what is going on here?" and determining to work it out. The concept of "the point of no return," the idea of "the static enneagram," and all of the examples – including their correlations with the strategy board – are entirely new work. The most significant examples are probably the enneagram of the Trinity and the cycle of reflection and action although the analyses of contemporary politics and the church year proved worthwhile, and the analysis of retail road vehicles has proved to be a remarkably reliable "first big clue" to an individual's home base on the strategy board.

Extravagant claims have been made for the wider potential of "the enneagram": made but never substantiated. Appendix 1 above uncovers and makes available some of that wider potential.

Nine types

The "desert fathers" were the third- and fourth-century forebears of all Christian religious orders. Their extensive theological work comes down to us in our contemporary understanding of Christ and the Trinity – and in the list of "seven deadly sins," derived from their work on human "passions" or motivations – full of insight into the human condition.

It was Oscar Ichazo in the 1960s who first brought together Gurdjieff's diagram, the list of seven-plus-two deadly sins, and the concept of "types" of people.

This work was developed by Claudio Naranjo from 1970 onward as a "personality typology" – within a context defined by particular theories in psychoanalysis.

Robert Ochs SJ took Naranjo's material and developed it specifically for use in spiritual direction – which represents a return to the original purpose of the material as developed by the desert fathers.

From Naranjo and Ochs onward the material is taken up by dozens of different authors with a whole range of perspectives and objectives – some following Ochs into practical Christian spiritual direction, others following Naranjo into the culture of personality typologies, psychodynamic theory, and psychoanalysis.

For most authors the nine "personality types" form the heart of the enneagram system, and the nine types are "endlessly described" in the literature – usually in long lists of characteristics with anecdotes and examples to illustrate each type.

Despite this, there has been no formal consensus on the core definition for each type. It is testimony to the resilience of the system that the types generally emerge in a recognizable form from one author to the next.

Attempts that have been made to define the "essence" of each type have tended to focus on a negative – on the type's "core sin" or "neediness" or "psychodynamic dysfunction." These are not good ways to define what it is to be human. The opposite approach – defining in terms of the gifts – also fails to explain the full complexity of the types – or the state of the world.

The present author's work began as a search for the one essential defining characteristic for each of the nine types in turn.

The concept of the strategy emerged to fill that role.

It began as a marginal note for just one of the nine types: "the strategy seems to be…"

Over time it became clear that all of the key features – good, bad, and indifferent – for each of the nine types in turn could be traced back to a single strategy, used by individuals of that type for engaging with the world around. The strategy becomes the defining essence of each type, describing and explaining all of each type's "essential" characteristics – corrupt and redeemed, effective and ineffective – from a starting point both morally and practically neutral.

The concept of the strategy brings an attractive and powerful simplicity to the system.

It also defines very clearly what the system is about. It is about how individuals engage with the world. It is not primarily about internal processes or psychodynamics or the self in isolation. It is not even primarily about "personality" – however that might be defined. It is very specifically "about" just one thing: how individuals meet the world and interact with it – and so in turn it is about actual temptations faced, and actual gifts used, out there in the world, where it counts.

The wings and the outer circle

Among the various authors, the arrangement of the nine types in a circle is universally acknowledged. It is explained by some variation of "wings" theory: that NINEs tend to have a bit of EIGHT in them, or a bit of ONE, or possibly both, and so on around the board; and that this is more pronounced than any other mixing of the types.

Once again this is presented as information without explanation.

The explanation lies hidden elsewhere in the literature: in the three "centers" or zones.

Authors are constantly looking for patterns and groupings within the list of nine types in order to categorize, simplify, and increase understanding. The most widely acknowledged pattern within the list is the division into three groups of three – under the headings of "head" and "heart" and "gut."

Descriptions given for "head" and "heart" and "gut" are often extraordinarily strained, being derived not from the plain meaning of the words but from an attempt to spot – for example – what FIVE and SIX and SEVEN might have in common: any strained form of words to link the three together is then labeled "head."

The present author was able to revisit the head and heart and gut classifications in the light of the newly identified strategies.

"Think it through first" for FIVE, "stick with what you know" for SIX, and "stay positive come what may" for SEVEN, do indeed sound like "head" choices.

"Give and care" for TWO, "lead and achieve" for THREE, and "be true to yourself" for FOUR, do indeed sound like heart-influenced choices.

Many authors find "gut" a difficult category, and speak of "body" or even "belly" – but "test people out" for EIGHT, "keep it simple" for NINE, and "be on your best behavior" for ONE, now identify the underlying nature of these types: they are strategies based on "gut instincts" or "gut reactions."

The head zone, the heart zone, and the gut zone are no longer awkwardly defined enneagram "super-categories": they are now defined by the natural meanings of the words "head" and "heart" and "gut" – head and heart as the classic inner rivals, plus gut as in "gut instinct" and "gut reaction."

More importantly, each one has been identified as the origin of the three strategies in its zone. We are firstly head types and heart types and gut types: we adopt one of the three strategies available in our zone, and everything else follows from there. Head and heart and gut come to form the foundation of the entire system.

And yet it remains to be explained why there should be three distinct strategies available in each zone, why each individual should choose the one they choose, and why each strategy should have its particular "wings" – sometimes the other two strategies in the same zone, but more often not.

For this author, the answer to all of this was staring out of the diagram – and yet it is found nowhere else in the literature. The answer lies in the idea of the secondary influence.

In the gut zone, it is the presence of a secondary influence that differentiates EIGHT and ONE from NINE. The strategy of EIGHT – "test people out" – is fundamentally a gut-plus-head strategy. And the strategy of ONE – "be on your best behavior" – is fundamentally a gut-plus-heart strategy. Head influence is not just on the SEVEN wing of EIGHT – it is in the very essence of EIGHT itself. And heart influence is not just on the TWO wing of ONE – it is in the very essence of ONE itself. It is this secondary influence that sets EIGHT and ONE apart from each other, and sets them apart from the all-gut-influenced NINE. In each zone the same principle applies – producing three distinct strategies in each zone.

Each strategy is now recognized as the consequence of one particular blend of influences from head and heart and gut. From this comes the explanation for the wings: they represent minor variations in that usual balance of head and heart and gut.

The nine strategies – and the pattern of the wings – now emerge from an entirely new "first principle" of the enneagram: that everything in the system can be traced back directly to the interaction of head and heart and gut as the individual engages with the world.

The brain and the end of rotational symmetry

Every enneagram author is looking for correlations with other theories or systems.

The acceptance of the "natural" meanings for head and heart and gut pointed this author toward the discoveries in neurology concerning the differential development of functions in different parts of the brain.

In the majority of human adults, the left side of the brain is differentially adapted for language and logic and reason – and the right side for emotions and images and dreams.

And there it is on the diagram: head on the left, heart on the right.

And then this further connection: that the rear or lower brain is the place of gut instinct and gut reaction.

From the enneagram there emerged a remarkably accurate map of the human brain – not just zone by zone but sector by sector: the frontal lobe functions of abstract thought, for example, are properly represented at FOUR and FIVE.

Making the connection with the human brain led to further insights into the diagram itself.

Head and heart together belong to the category of "inner life" – even though they are rivals within it – in a way that "gut" does not.

Looking again at all nine types, it is possible to identify a continuous vertical scale in this circular diagram – from the direct instinct and intuition of the gut zone at the top to the inner life of head and heart at the bottom.

The three-phase rotational symmetry of the diagram has been supplemented by a major left-right contrast and a vertical scale.

Head versus Heart takes this entirely new supplementary reading of the diagram as fundamental to the system – from the top of page one.

Nine arrows

The distinctive irregular pattern of the arrows within the outer circle has been the biggest mystery of the enneagram – and some authors have shied away from it for precisely that reason.

A list of nine types seems logical enough – especially when grouped as three sets of three under the headings of head and heart and gut. But with head and heart and gut viewed as three interchangeable alternatives, the diagram has three phases of rotational symmetry – and there is no justification for the pattern of nine arrows taking anything other than a rotationally symmetrical form.

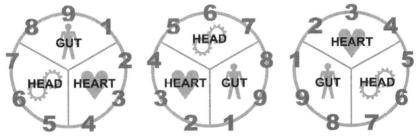

Some writers reject the pattern of the arrows entirely on this basis. Others speak guardedly of "the general direction of the arrows" – by which they mean the alternative pattern of three equilateral triangles that others have more explicitly proposed. Only two small changes are required: you replace the arrows FOUR-TWO and FIVE-SEVEN with FOUR-SEVEN and FIVE-TWO; the other seven arrows can be left unchanged.

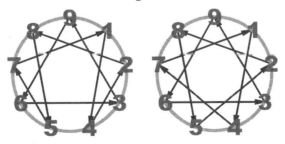

And yet those irregular two – FOUR-TWO and FIVE-SEVEN – seem to describe real human lives with all the same insight and value as the other seven "more regular" lines across the board – and the two proposed alternative lines do not. So how can the pattern be justified? Why is it the way that it is?

Uncovering the logic of the pattern of the arrows went hand in hand with "undoing" the rotational symmetry of head and heart and gut – recognizing instead the left-right symmetry of head and heart and the vertical scale from "gut" to "inner life".

As well as emphasizing the stark separation of head and heart, the irregular horseshoe shape of the hexagon encourages the idea that the gut zone is both generally more accessible and somehow central to the whole project – which indeed it is. The gut zone represents direct interaction with the world around – and "interaction with the world around" is precisely what the nine strategies are all about.

The circle and the triangle, meanwhile, keep the faith with the simultaneous alternative reading whereby there are indeed three influences interacting as interchangeable alternatives.

This general "justification by overview" was eventually supplemented by a detailed explanation of how each arrow works – in each direction: eighteen potential "moves" in all – described in full in the main text as "Moves across the board," with additional material in Appendix 1 above.

Conclusion

For the first time *Head versus Heart* lays open the underlying logical structure of the enneagram.

It explains why the nine types exist as they do, why they can be arranged around a circle in a specific order, and why they interconnect to form a distinctive irregular pattern of internal lines.

We cannot know how much of this underlying logic was understood by Gurdjieff and Ichazo or how much they were simply "going by instinct" – but the underlying logic of the system has been uncovered, and the system is sound.

The Strategy Board is a powerful system "for understanding both yourself and other people."

Its assumptions are the assumptions of faith: that when we speak of the experience of humankind we must speak of sin and redemption, of temptations and gifts, and of participation in the community of Christ.

It is fundamentally outward looking – concerned with the nature of our engagement with the world, with recognizing and valuing the gifts of others, and with discerning our own vocation in the world.

It is logical and rational throughout – with clear links to cognitive, behavioral, and even neurological psychology: the psychology of the mainstream scientific community.

It traces every detail of the system back to the simple familiar concepts of "head" and "heart" – plus "gut," as in "gut instinct" and "gut reaction."

It has plotted a map of humankind and a map of the spiritual journeys we make – that we might better understand ourselves and other people, discern our own vocation in the world, avoid the temptations around us, and grow in the grace of our God-given gifts.

Sources and resources

Writers in the Jesuit tradition of Robert Ochs

All of these writers belong in different ways to the Jesuit enneagram tradition of Robert Ochs:

Maria Beesing, Robert Nogosek, and Patrick O'Leary, *The Enneagram: a journey of self discovery* (Dimension, 1984). The earliest book in print.

Richard Rohr and Adreas Ebert, *Discovering the Enneagram: an ancient tool for a new spiritual journey* (Crossroad, 1990), now in a new edition *The Enneagram, A Christian Perspective* (Crossroad, 2001). An excellent compendium of Christian resources on the nine types.

Don Richard Riso and Russ Hudson, *The Wisdom of the Enneagram* (Bantam, 1999). The definitive textbook of Riso and Hudson's material. Written in accessible "secular" language but very much part of the Jesuit tradition.

Éilís Bergin and Eddie Fitzgerald, *An Enneagram Guide: a spirituality of love in brokenness* (SDB Media / Twenty-Third Publications / Bayard, 1993). Catholic resources from the Irish Republic.

Writers in other enneagram traditions

Using the same distinctive diagram but taking different routes in the development of the material – great rivals of each other and of the Jesuit tradition:

Helen Palmer, *The Enneagram: understanding yourself and the others in your life* (HarperCollins, 1988). Material derived directly from Naranjo, not via Ochs. "Psychodynamic therapy" rather than "spiritual direction."

Anthony George Edward Blake, *The Intelligent Enneagram* (Shambhala, 1996). In the Gurdjieff tradition rejecting any connection with nine types of people – and extraordinarily obscure.

The author is available
for leading seminars, workshops,
quiet days and retreats
on this material

www.michaelhampson.co.uk